GYMNASTIC ACTIVITIES • DA

PE LESSON PLANS

reception COMPLETE TEACHING PROGRAMME

SECOND EDITION

LEAPFROGS

JIM HALL

A music CD with tracks to accompany many of the Dance Lessons in this series is available separately (ISBN: 978 07136 7902 1).

Relevant tracks are indicated on each lesson page with the following logo:

Published in 2009 by A & C Black Publishers Ltd
36 Soho Square, London W1D 3QY
www.acblack.com

ISBN 978 14081 0990 8

A CIP record for this book is available from the British Library.

Note: While every effort has been made to ensure that the content of this book is as technically accurate and as sound as possible, neither the author nor the publisher can accept responsibility for any injury or loss sustained as a result of the use of this material.

A & C Black uses paper produced with elemental chlorine-free pulp, harvested from managed sustainable forests.

Acknowledgements
Cover illustration by Tom Croft
Cover design by James Watson
Illustrations by Jan Smith

Typeset in 10pt DIN Regular.

Printed and bound in Great Britain by Martins the Printers, Berwick upon Tweed.

Contents

Introduction

Because an increasing number of young children today do not have the opportunity to take part in regular play, physical activity or exercise, enjoyable, vigorous, well taught physical education lessons are more important than ever. Equally important is a sense of staff unity regarding the 'Why?', the 'What?', and the 'How?' of physical education to deliver a whole school, successful programme with continuity and high standards from year to year.

The main reasons for teaching physical education, include:

Physical development. First and foremost, the main reason for teaching physical education has always been to inspire vigorous, enjoyable, challenging and wholehearted physical activity that develops normal healthy growth and satisfactory development of each pupil's strength, suppleness and stamina. The skills taught also aim to develop skilful, confident, well-controlled and safe movement. It is hoped that the varied skills will give pleasure and satisfaction, catering for many interests and aptitudes, and will eventually enable pupils to take part in healthy, worthwhile and sociable activities long after they have left school. These skills, learned and enjoyed at school, are remembered by the body for a very long time.

Personal, social and emotional development, compensating for the near total disappearance of play in the out-of-school lives of many of our pupils. It is reported that millions of children spend most of their free time – up to five hours every day – watching a TV or a computer screen. It has also been claimed that parents, who refuse to let their children go out to play, are producing a 'battery-farmed' generation who will never become resilient and will be unable to deal with risk.

This lack of play means no exercise, no fresh air, no physical development, no social development though interaction with others, no adventure in challenging situations and no emotional development. It has been said 'an individual's regard for, and attitude to, his or her physical self, especially at primary school age, is important to the development of self-image and the value given to self.' Physical education lessons are extremely visual, providing many opportunities for demonstrating success, creativity, versatility and enthusiastic performances which should be recognised by the teacher, praised and commented upon, and shared with others who should be encouraged to be warm in their praise and comments. Such successes can enhance a pupil's feelings of pride and self-confidence.

The play-like nature of physical education lessons is obvious. In games, running, jumping and landing, throwing and catching, batting, skipping, trying to score points or goals; in gymnastic activities, running, jumping and landing, rolling, climbing, swinging on ropes, balancing, circling on bars; and in dance, skipping, running and jumping, travelling with a partner, a group or a circle in performing a dance, are all playful actions in which pupils find fun and satisfaction from performing well, and social development from being in the company of others.

When teaching physical education lessons now, teachers need to remember that the lessons may be providing the only active play that some of the pupils will experience that week. The lessons must be vigorous, enjoyable, and give an impression of children at play.

Contributing to pupils' health now, and long after they have left school. The health of our children and eventually the health of our nation, has been a cause for concern for university researchers and health experts for decades. A 1997 headline described British children as 'The Flab Generation'. It was estimated in 2000, that in a class of thirty children, two will go on to have a heart attack, three will develop diabetes, and thirteen will become obese, all as result of a sedentary lifestyle and a diet dominated by chips, biscuits, sweets and sugary drinks. A 2002 report revealed that a third of 10 year olds did not even walk continuously for ten minutes a week.

The above statistics and figures have become far worse since those early ignored warnings. The NHS treated 85,000 patients for clinical obesity in 2007 and it is estimated that by 2020, 50% of all children in Britain will be obese. England has the fastest growing weight problem in Europe. The link between obesity and diabetes is well known and 100,000 UK patients are diagnosed with type 2 diabetes every year, fuelled by the nation's obesity problem. Douglas Smallwood, Chief Executive of the charity Diabetes UK says 'Diabetes is a serious condition which can lead to devastating complications such as blindness, amputation, heart and kidney disease.' Almost one hundred diabetics a week have a limb amputated because of complications with their disease.

An extra twelve kilograms in weight boosts the risk of cancer by 50%. Coronary heart disease causes 105,000 deaths a year and 2.6 million people are thought to be living with the symptoms of heart disease. Scientists have warned that unfit, lazy children are six times more likely to develop early signs of heart disease than those who are active and take exercise. For the first time, experts have established that activity levels in children as young as seven can have a serious effect on their future health. Professor Paul Gately, of Leeds Metropolitan University says 'Inactive children at a relatively young age are already storing up health risks for the future.' Health specialists, concerned for the health of our nation, are now repeatedly emphasising the importance of regular exercise as the best way to reduce the risks of suffering life-threatening illnesses in later life.

The National Obesity Forum has called for urgent action to tackle the obesity problem which, they calculate, causes 30,000 deaths each year and emphasises that the time to act is in childhood before irreversible damage has been done, and while lifelong habits can be learned. British Heart Foundation research found that taking 30 minutes of moderate exercise most days reduces the risk of an early death by more than a quarter. Diabetes UK warns that obesity is making a diabetes epidemic inevitable. Physical activity and a sensible diet are the best ways to reduce the risk of developing diabetes. The World Cancer Research Fund 2007 Report, produced by scientists and medical experts from around the world, tells us that most cancers are preventable by choosing a healthy diet, being physically active and maintaining a healthy weight. They recommend being physically active for at least 30 minutes every day, to keep the heart healthy and to reduce the risk of cancer.

Realistically, it is only in schools in physical education lessons, that we can encourage and help children to succeed in a wide range of physical skills and inspire, motivate and facilitate a joy in physical activity that will combat the health problems mentioned above. Physical education makes a unique contribution to an all-round, balanced education, but it also makes a special contribution to a life-prolonging, healthy lifestyle. For today's primary school children regular, excellent, vigorous and enjoyable physical education lessons are probably the best health products they will ever receive.

Teaching Physical Education

The teacher of physical education, almost uniquely, works alone and unaided, and is involved in whole class teaching with no help from the mass of teaching aids that help to keep pupils purposefully and often independently engaged in their classrooms. Even if he or she is talking to an individual, a pair or a small group, the teacher in a physical education lesson still needs to be aware of the whole class and how it is responding to the set task.

The teacher is the source and inspiration for everything that happens in the lessons. He or she needs to be well prepared to make the lesson complete, enjoyable, stimulating and challenging; enthusiastic to create an equally enthusiastic response; warm and encouraging to help pupils feel pleased and good about themselves; and intensely interested in inspiring vigorous physical activity in pupils, many of whom, away from school, may have inactive and sedentary lifestyles.

The lesson plan is the teacher's essential guide and reminder of the current lesson's content. Failure to plan and record lessons results in the same or similar things being done, month after month. Parts of the lesson gradually disappear, and an unprepared teacher can finish up doing no teaching in a lesson where everything is vague or has been done before. Pupils at apparatus in such an unprepared lesson answer 'Nothing' when asked 'What has your group been asked to do at this apparatus?'

July's lesson will only be at a more advanced stage that the previous September's if all the lessons in between have been recorded and referred to, to make each succeeding lesson move on and introduce new, interesting and exciting challenges. The lesson usually runs for four or five weeks (one lesson per week) to give the class enough time to practise, improve, develop, learn, remember and enjoy all the skills involved.

'Dead spots' and queue avoidance. The 'scenes of busy activity' which every physical education lesson should be requires an understanding by all pupils that they should be 'found working, not waiting'. This means that they need to be trained to respond immediately, behave well, keep on practising until stopped, and avoid standing immobile in queues.

The teacher needs to avoid talking the class out of their lesson through over-long explanations, demonstrations and pupil reflections following demonstrations. Lessons that lose a lot of time result in unsatisfactory, hurried apparatus work, frustratingly short time for playing games, and half-created dances with no time to share them proudly, with the class.

Demonstrations and observations by pupils and teacher are essential teaching aids because we remember what we see – good quality work; safe, correct ways to perform; the exact meanings of physical education terminology; and good examples of variety and interesting contrasts. All can watch one, two or a small group. Half of the class can watch the other half. Each can watch a partner. These occasional demonstrations, with comments by the observing pupils, often bring out good points not noticed by the teacher; train pupils to understand the elements of 'movement'; and let teachers ask 'how can it be improved?' Making friendly, encouraging, helpful points to classmates is good for class morale and for extending the class repertoire in physical education. ('Occasional' means once or twice at most in one lesson because of the time taken to do this.)

Further class practice should always follow a demonstration so that everyone can try to include some of the good features praised and commented on.

Shared choice or **indirect teaching** takes place when the teacher decides the nature of the activity and challenges the class to decide on the actions. Limits set are determined by the experience of the pupils. From the simple 'Can you travel on the apparatus, using your hands and feet?' with its slight limitations, we can progress on to 'Can you travel on the apparatus, using hands and feet, and include a still balance, a direction change, and taking all the weight on your hands at some point?'

Shared choice teaching produces a wide variety of results to add to the class repertoire. Being creative is extremely satisfying and most primary school pupils enjoy and are capable of making individual responses.

Direct teaching takes place when the teacher tells the class what to do, including, for example: any of the traditional gymnastic skills; the way to hold, throw and catch a ball; or how to do a folk dance step. Correct, safe ways to move; support yourself; grip, lift and carry apparatus; and throw implements, are all directly taught.

If the class is restless, not responding, or doing poor work, a directed activity can restore interest and discipline and provide ideas and a valuable starting point from which to develop. Pupils who are less interested, less inventive or less gifted physically, will benefit from direct teaching, particularly if the teacher can suggest an alternative, simpler but equally acceptable idea. 'If you do not like rolling forwards, try rolling sideways instead. Start, curled up on your back, with your hands clasped under your knees. This keeps your head out of the way.' The occasional stimulus of a direct request is the kind of challenge many pupils enjoy, and they respond enthusiastically. 'Can you and your partner bat the small ball up and down between you, six times?'

Motivational teaching. Children say that the things that motivate them to take part in physical activities are fun and skill development. They want to enjoy, learn and succeed. The more philosophical among them might also add that feelings of happiness are associated with having something to look forward to; to enjoy; and then to remember with pleasure (and often with pride). This anticipation, realisation and retrospect-inspiring potential of excellent physical education lessons and activities, makes it the favourite subject for many primary school pupils.

Safe Practice and Accident Prevention

In physical education lessons, where a main aim is to contribute to normal, healthy growth and physical development, we must do everything possible to avoid accidents.

Good supervision by the teacher is key to safe practice. He or she must be there with the class at all times, and teaching from positions from which the majority of the class can be seen. This usually means circulating on the outside looking in, with no-one behind his or her back. Good teaching develops skilful, well-controlled, safe movement with pupils wanting to avoid others to ensure that they have space to practise and perform well and not be impeded in any way. The outward expression of this caring attitude we are trying to create is the sensible, unselfish sharing of hall floor space, apparatus and playground, and self-control in avoiding others.

Badly behaved classes who do not respond immediately, or start or stop as requested; who rush around selfishly and noisily disturbing others; who are never quiet in their tongues or body movements; and who do not try to move well, are destructive of any prospects for high standards or lesson enjoyment by the majority and the teacher. A safe environment requires a well-behaved, quiet, attentive and responsive class. Good behaviour must be continually pursued until it becomes the normal, expected way to work in every lesson. There is nothing to talk about, apart from those occasions when comments are requested after a demonstration, or when partners are quietly discussing their response to a challenge.

The hall should be at a good working temperature with windows and doors opened or closed to cope with changing seasons and central heating variations. Potentially dangerous chairs, tables, trolleys, piano or television should be removed or pushed against a wall or into a corner. Floor sockets for receiving securing pins for ropes and climbing frames should be regularly cleared of cleaning substances which harden and block the small sockets.

In playground games lessons, pupils must be trained to remain inside the lines of the grids or netball courts and to avoid running, chasing or dodging into fences, walls, sheds, seats, hutted classrooms, or steps into buildings. In any 'tag' games, pupils must be told 'Touch the person you have caught very gently, never pushing them or causing them to fall or stumble.'

Before the lesson, the teacher checks for sensible, safe clothing with no watches, rings or jewellery whose impact against another child can cause serious scarring or injury; no long trousers that catch heels; no long sleeves that catch thumbs, impeding safe gripping; and no long, un-bunched hair that impedes vision. Indoors, barefoot work is recommended because it is quiet, provides a safe, strong grip on apparatus, enhances the appearance of the work, and enables the little-used muscles of feet and ankles to develop as they grip, balance, support, propel and receive the body weight.

In teaching gymnastic activities, the following safety considerations are important:

○ In floor and apparatus work, pupils need to be taught the correct, safe, 'squashy' landing after a jump so that they land safely on the balls of the feet, with ankles, knees and hips 'giving' without jarring.

○ When inverted, with all the weight on their hands, pupils need to be taught to keep fingers pointing forward, arms straight and strong, and head looking forward, not back under arms. Looking back under the arms makes everything appear to be upside down.

○ On climbing frames, pupils must be told 'Fingers grip over the bar, thumbs grip under the bar, always, for a safe, strong grip.'

A Suggested Way to Start a First Lesson with a New Class

Unless taught otherwise, pupils travel round the hall or the playground in an anti-clockwise circle, all following the person in front of them. If one pupil slows down or stops suddenly, the next can bump into that person, possibly knocking him or her over, causing an angry upset and a disturbance.

By travelling and confining themselves within this circle, a class fails to use all the possible room or playground space, depriving themselves of enough space to travel freely in different directions, and to join several actions together, on the spot or travelling about. Also, with everyone travelling round in a circle, sometimes side by side, pairs of less well-behaved pupils can be so close together that their poor behaviour, expressed in talking, not listening, slow responses, and noisy, poor performances, completely upsets the teacher's aim to give the class an enjoyable, lively, quiet, thoughtful and co-operative start to the lesson and the year's programme.

By continually making the whole class listen for the signal 'Stop!', we force them to pay attention, listen, and respond quickly.

Suggested pre-start to the lesson

1 Please show me your very best walking...go! Visit every part of the room, the sides, the ends, corners, as well as the middle. Swing your arms strongly and step out smartly.

2 When I call 'Stop!', show me how quickly you can stop and stand perfectly still. Keep walking smartly and visiting all parts of the room. Stop! Stand still!

3 If you are standing too near a piece of apparatus, like Ben by the piano, or too near someone else, like Leroy and Emily, please take one step into a big space all by yourself. Go!

4 When you start walking this time, travel along straight lines, never following anyone. If you find yourself behind someone, change direction and continue along a new straight line, following no-one. Ready? Go!

5 Come on. March briskly and smartly and pretend you are leaving footprints in every part of the room. When I call 'Stop!' you will stop immediately and then take a step into your own space if you are near apparatus or another person. Stop!

6 In our next practice, listen for my 'Stop!' and show me that no-one is standing behind another person, looking towards that person's back, following them. Go!

7 Stop! Stand still, after moving onto your own space if necessary. Now show your very best running, with the emphasis on lifting your heels, knees and hands to keep your running soft, silent and strong – and, of course, travelling along straight lines, never following anyone.

8 Stop! Be still! This half of the class stand with feet apart, arms folded, to watch this other half doing their very best running. Look out for and tell me later about anyone whose running you liked and be able to tell me what you liked about it. The running half...ready...go! Do not pick anyone who is following someone, or anyone who is not lifting heels, knees or arms strongly. Please watch carefully.

9 Stop! Watchers, whose running did you like. Yes, Liam?

10 I (Liam) liked Nathalie's running because she used her eyes well, looking for spaces, and she seemed to float along beautifully and easily, with heels, knees and hands being lifted high.

11 Thank you very much, Liam, for that excellent answer. Now let's look at Nathalie to see and learn from the good things mentioned by Liam. Please run again, Nathalie.

12 (Repeat with the other half working and the other half observing and commenting.)

Headings When Considering Standards in Physical Education

Physical Education lessons are so visual that most of the following headings can be considered by an interested observer.

- **Vigorous physical activity**, involving all pupils for most of the lesson, is the most important feature of an excellent lesson.

- **Responsive pupils, behaving well and obviously enjoying lessons**; working hard to learn and improve skills; and exuding enthusiasm and concentration, are an uplifting feature of high standards.

- **Enthusiastic teaching, using praise and encouragement warmly**, stimulates pupils to even greater levels of endeavour. Praise is specific, referring to what is pleasing, to inform the pupil being praised and to let others hear and learn. 'Well done, Charlotte. Your balances are still, firm and beautifully stretched.'

- **Skills, appropriate to the age group**, are taught and developed. There is an impression of skilful, quiet, confident, well-controlled, successful performing with economy of effort. Pupils show understanding by their ability to remember and repeat their movements.

- **Pupils' behaviour towards one another is excellent**. Undressing and dressing quickly to extend lesson time; safe, unselfish sharing of space and apparatus; working quietly to avoid lessons being stopped because of noise; observing demonstrations with interest and then making helpful, friendly comments; and co-operating well as partners and members of groups and teams, all indicate desirable standards of behaviour.

- **Varied teaching styles include**:

  a   indirect or shared choice teaching

  b   direct teaching

  c   good and varied use of demonstrations, observations, comments.

- **Satisfactory time allocation** provides regular, weekly lessons in dance, games and gymnastic activities – a broad programme which also includes athletic activities and swimming for Juniors.

- **Lesson plans** are in evidence, as a reminder of all parts of the current lesson, and as a reminder of what has been taught, so that the work can be progressed, month by month, throughout the year.

- **Sensibly dressed pupils** wear shorts, a T shirt or blouse, and plimsolls. Indoors, barefoot work is recommended. As an example, the teacher should at least change into appropriate footwear.

- **Continuity and progression from year to year** are evident in the way that older pupils work harder for longer at increasingly difficult activities, demonstrating skill and versatility.

- **An awareness of safe practice and accident prevention** is evident in the way that pupils share the limited space. The correct way to lift, carry and use apparatus, land, move, roll, support and use the body generally, are regularly mentioned.

Gymnastic Activities

Introduction to Gymnastic Activities

Gymnastic Activities is the indoor lesson that includes varied floorwork on a clear floor, unimpeded by apparatus, followed by varied apparatus work which should take up just over half of the lesson time. Ideally, the portable apparatus will have been positioned around the sides and ends of the room, near to where it will be used, before lessons start in the morning or afternoon. This allows each of the seven or eight mixed infant groups, or the five or six mixed junior groups of pupils to lift, carry and position their apparatus in a very short time, because no set will need to be moved more than 3–5 metres. The lesson is traditionally of 30 minutes duration.

The following pages aim, first of all, to produce a sense of staff-room unity regarding the nature of good practice and high standards in teaching Gymnastic Activities lessons. Without this sense of unity among the teachers concerned, there is no continuity of aims, expectations or programme, and there will be a less than satisfactory level of achievement. Secondly, the following pages provide a full scheme of work for Gymnastic Activities. There is a lesson plan and accompanying pages of detailed explanatory notes for every month, designed to help teachers and schools with ideas for lessons that are progressive.

Why We Teach Gymnastic Activities

Ideally, the expressions of intent known as 'Aims' should represent the combined views of all the staff.

Aim 1 To inspire vigorous physical activity to promote normal healthy growth and physical development. Physical Education is most valuable when pupils' participation is enthusiastic, vigorous and wholehearted. All subsequent aims for a good programme depend on achieving this first aim.

Aim 2 To teach physical skills to develop skilful, well-controlled, versatile movement. We want pupils to enjoy moving well, safely and confidently. Physical Education makes a unique contribution to a child's physical development because the activities are experienced at first hand by doing them.

Aim 3 To help pupils become good learners as well as good movers. Knowledge, understanding and learning are achieved through a combination of doing, feeling and experiencing physical activity. Pupils are challenged to think for themselves, making decisions about their actions.

Aim 4 To develop pupils' self-confidence and self-esteem by appreciating the importance of physical achievement; by helping them to achieve; and by recognising and sharing such achievement with others.

Aim 5 To develop desirable social qualities, helping pupils get on well with one another by bringing them together in mutual endeavours. Friendly, co-operative, close relationships are an ever-present feature of Physical Education lessons.

Aim 6 To provide opportunities for exciting, almost adventurous actions (particularly climbing, swinging, balancing, jumping and landing) and vigorous exercise – seldom experienced away from school. We want our pupils to use these lessons as outlets for their energy and we want them to believe that exercise is good for you and your heart, and makes you feel and look better. We aim to encourage participation in a healthy lifestyle, long after pupils have left school.

The Gymnastic Activities Lesson Plan for Infants – 30 minutes

One answer to the question 'What do we teach in a gymnastic activities lesson?' might be – 'All the natural activities and ways of moving of which the body is capable and which, if practised safely and wholeheartedly, ensure normal healthy growth and physical development.'

It has been said that 'What you don't use, you lose.' Most pupils hardly ever strenuously use their natural capacity for vigorous running, jumping and landing from a height; rolling in different directions; balancing on a variety of body parts; upending to take their weight on their hands; gripping, climbing and swinging on a rope; hanging, swinging or circling on a bar; or whole body bending, stretching, arching and twisting. These natural movements and actions should be present in every gymnastic activities lesson, ensuring that pupils do not lose the ability to do them and that their physical development does not diminish.

A teacher's determination to inspire the class to use and not lose their natural physicality can be strengthened by observing how many children are collected in cars at the school gates. They are then transported home to their after school, house-bound, sedentary home lives.

Floorwork (12 minutes) starts the lesson and includes:

○ Activities for the legs, exploring and developing the many actions possible when travelling on feet, and ways to jump and land.

○ Activities for the body, including the many ways to bend, stretch, rock, roll, twist, curl, turn, and the ways in which body parts receive, support and transfer the body weight in travelling and balancing.

○ Activities for the arms and shoulders, the least used parts of our body. We strengthen them by using them to hold all or part of the body weight on the spot or moving. This strength is needed in gripping, climbing, hanging, swinging and circling, and in levering on to and across apparatus, supported by the hands alone.

Apparatus Work (16 minutes) is the climax of the lesson, making varied, unique and challenging demands on pupils whose whole body – legs, arms and shoulders, back and abdominal muscles – must work hard because of the more difficult tasks:

○ travelling on hands and feet, over, under, across and around obstacles, as well as vertically, often supported only on hands

○ jumping and landing from greater heights

○ rolling on to, along, from and across apparatus

○ balancing on high or narrow surfaces

○ upending to take all body weight on hands on apparatus above floor level

○ gripping, swinging, climbing and circling on ropes and bars.

Final Floor Activity (2 minutes) after the apparatus has been returned to its starting places around the sides, ends and corners of the hall, brings the whole class together again in a simple activity based on the lesson's main emphasis or theme. After the bustle of apparatus removal – the swishing of ropes along trackways, the creaking of climbing frames being wheeled away, the bumping of benches, planks, boxes and trestles – there is a quiet, calm, thoughtful and focused ending.

Three Ways to Teach Apparatus Work

1 **(Easiest Method) Pupils use all the apparatus freely, as they respond to tasks that relate to the lesson theme.** Several challenges provide non-stop apparatus work for infants and juniors. Pupils are stationary only when watching a demonstration, having a teaching point emphasised, or when being given the next task. This method is normally used with infant classes, because they are able to visit and use all pieces of apparatus, including their favourites – ropes and climbing frames.

   'Show me a still balance and beautifully stretched body shape on each piece of apparatus.' (Body shape awareness and balance)

   'Show me how you can approach each piece of apparatus going forward and leave going sideways.' (Space awareness – directions)

   'Leader, show your partner one touch only on each piece of apparatus, then off to the next piece.' (Partner work)

2 **Groups stay and work at one set of apparatus**. Repetition helps pupils improve and remember a series of linked actions. The task is the same for all groups, based on the lesson theme.

   'Make your hands important in arriving on, and your feet important in leaving the apparatus.' (Body parts awareness)

   'Can you include swings on to and off apparatus; a swing into a roll; and a swing to take all the weight on your hands?' (Swinging)

   'Travel from opposite sides, up to, on, along and from the apparatus, to finish in your partner's starting place.' (Partner work)

   Groups rotate to the next apparatus after about five minutes and will work at three sets in a lesson, rotating clockwise one lesson, and anti-clockwise the next, to meet all apparatus every two lessons.

3 **Each group practises a different, specific skill on each piece of apparatus – balancing, rolling, climbing, for example**. This method of teaching is more difficult than the other two because it needs more technical knowledge, and because the teacher is giving five or six sets of instructions instead of one. As it is a direct challenge to 'skills hungry' pupils, it is very popular.

   Benches 'At upturned benches, slowly balance and walk forward. Look straight ahead. Feel for the bench before you step on it.'

   Ropes 'Grip strongly with hands together and feet crossed. Can you take one hand off, while swinging, to prove a good foot grip?'

   Low cross box 'A face vault is like a high bunny jump to cross the box, as you twist over, facing the box top all the way.'

   Climbing frames 'Travel by moving hands only, then feet only.'

   Mats 'Roll sideways with body curled small and then with body long and stretched' (log roll).

   Groups rotate to the next piece of apparatus after about five minutes, rotating clockwise one lesson, and anti-clockwise the next lesson, meeting all apparatus every two lessons.

Organising Groups for Infant School Apparatus Work

The recommended system for ensuring that apparatus can be lifted, carried and placed in position, quickly and easily, needs the co-operation of all the teachers. Before lessons start in the morning or afternoon, the portable apparatus is placed around the sides and ends of the hall near to where it will be used. Each group of pupils will thus only have to carry it 2–3 metres. A well-trained class can have the apparatus in place in 30 seconds. After all lessons are finished each day, as much of the apparatus as possible should remain in the hall, in corners, against or on the platform, or at the sides and ends of the room. Mats can be stored vertically behind climbing frames, benches and boxes.

Groups of four pupils are appropriate for infant school apparatus work and the organisation into the seven or eight groups is done in the first lesson in September. Pupils are told 'These are your groups and starting places for apparatus work.' For the four or five lessons, the same groups go to the same starting places, becoming expert in lifting, carrying and placing their apparatus. At the start of the school year, groups are taught how to lift, carry and place the various pieces of apparatus. For example, at a bench, box or nesting table group, 'Stand, one at each end and one at each side. Bend your knees, put your hands under your side of the apparatus with arms straight. Stand up and lift carefully. Carry it to here, please, then bend your knees to put it down quietly.' The teacher shows them a position, a few metres away from where they started. 'Liam and Nathalie, please bring your mat now, and put it beside the bench.'

At the end of the lesson, the class is asked to go and stand beside the apparatus they brought out. After the apparatus has been returned to its starting places at the sides or ends of the room, groups should be praised for the 'quiet, safe and sensible way you all moved your apparatus' and reminded 'Please remember your own starting place for apparatus next week.'

Positioning of Apparatus During Lessons

The teacher needs to provide varied actions and physical demands as pupils progress from apparatus to apparatus, meeting a challenging, interesting series of settings. The typical spread of eight or nine simple sets of apparatus might include:

- bench and mat
- trestle, inclined plank and mat
- ropes frame
- nesting table and mat
- bottom section of box and mat
- bench and mat
- two trestles, plank to link trestles and mat
- climbing frames
- top section of two-section box and mat
- pyramid boxes, linking plank and mats

A safe environment is ensured by providing:

- mats where pupils are expected to land from a height
- mats that are well away from walls, windows, doors or other obstacles such as a piano, trolley chairs, and well away from the landing areas of adjacent apparatus
- height and width of apparatus that are appropriate for the age of the class – not too narrow to balance on, and not too high to jump from.

Mats are used to cushion a landing from a height and to roll on. We do not use mats under ropes or around climbing frames because we do not ask pupils to jump down from a height. If mats are at climbing frames, pupils often behave in a foolhardy way, enticed into dangerous jumping.

Fixed and portable apparatus

Apparatus referred to in the lesson plans that follow, and shown in the examples of simple and larger apparatus groupings, include the following items:

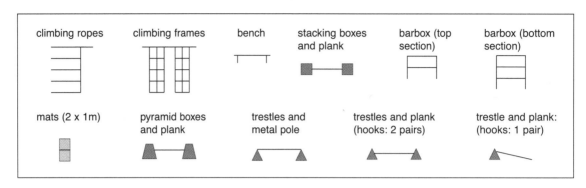

- ❍ 12 mats 2 × 1 m

- ❍ 3 benches

- ❍ 1 barbox that can be divided into two smaller boxes by lifting off the top section. The lower section should have a platform top

- ❍ 1 pair stacking boxes, 48 × 48 cm base, 33 cm high; and one 2.4 m plank

- ❍ 1 pair pyramid boxes, 78 cm high, 60 cm long, 53 cm wide at base tapering to 38 cm wide at top, and one 2.4 m plank

- ❍ 1 pair of 1 m, 1.06 m, 1.4 m trestles

- ❍ 2 planks with two pairs of hooks

- ❍ 2 planks with one pair of hooks

- ❍ 1 3 m metal pole

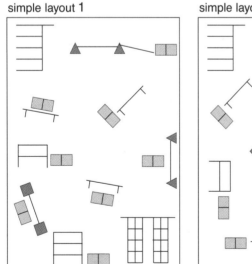

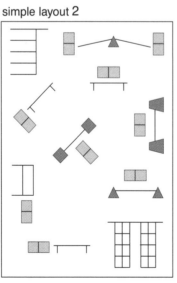

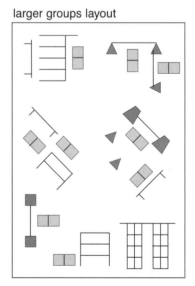

The Use of Themes in Teaching Gymnastic Activities

Week after week, month after month, the teacher and class come into the school hall and see the same apparatus, apparently offering the same limited set of activities every time. In dance, we continually move on to learning and performing new dances and building a huge repertoire. In games, the new seasons bring their different sports and the varied games implements provide an interesting and exciting range – including new games created by the teacher and pupils.

Gymnastic activities lessons are made different through applying a new idea, emphasis or theme each month. We do not simply 'do' the basic action. We do it, focusing on a particular aspect of movement, to improve in understanding and versatility, as well as in competence. A theme is a particular aspect of movement chosen by the teacher as a focal point around which to build a series of lessons.

At the very beginning of the series of four or five lessons during which an individual lesson is repeated, it is recommended that the pupils are 'put in the picture' regarding their lesson's main aims or emphases. In cases where they are going to be assessed on the outcome of the lesson, it is essential to explain to them what new skills, knowledge and understanding they will be expected to demonstrate. Identifying the lesson theme or main emphasis to the class is also a way for the teacher to put him or herself 'in the picture' about the main objectives of the lesson and to focus on them.

Start of year themes with a new class will have an emphasis on good behaviour; sensible, safe sharing of floor and apparatus space; immediate responses to commands and challenges set by the teacher; establishing a tradition of wholehearted, vigorous effort and a co-operative attitude towards one's classmates; and co-operating with others to lift, carry and place apparatus quietly, sensibly and safely.

A suggested set of six progressive themes for a month to month programme

1 **Body parts awareness** for better controlled, safer, more correct activity. 'Show me varied ways to travel, using one foot, both feet, or one foot after the other.'

2 **Body shape awareness** for improved poise, better posture and firmer body tension. 'Can you run and jump up high with feet together and long, straight legs?'

3 **Space awareness** for improved variety, quality and interest, and safer practising. 'Can you travel all round the room, using feet only, sometimes going forwards, and sometimes sideways?'

4 **Effort awareness** for more interesting contrasts, better quality and stronger work. 'As you travel in a variety of ways can you include actions that are small, light and gentle, and actions that are large, lively and strong?'

5 **Sequences** for longer, harder, versatile work, stamping it with own personality. 'Make up a sequence you can remember, of three or four joined-up actions and changing body shapes on different body parts.' (Standing, kneeling, lying, sitting, upended on shoulders, arched on back or front.)

6 **Partner work** for new, enjoyable, sociable, more demanding experiences not possible on one's own, and to extend movement understanding because you need to recognise partner's actions. 'Stand, facing each other. Can you, with a little bend of knees as a start signal, bounce at the same speed? Can you do opposites, with one going up as the other comes down?'

Progressing Gymnastic Activities over the 4 or 5 weeks of the Lesson's Development

Using 'Stepping' as an example of an activity to be developed

Lessons 1 and 2

a   Concentrate on the **'What?'**, the actions, their correct form, and how the body parts concerned are working.

'Can you step quietly and neatly, visiting all parts of the room? Travel on straight lines, never following anyone.'

'Which parts of the foot can support you? Tip toes, insides or outsides? Long or short steps or a mixture?'

'Can you vary the idea of stepping, not always passing your feet?' (Chasse, crossover, toes down and swing.)

b   Insist on good, clear body shapes to make everything look better and be more demanding.

'Step out nice and tall as you travel. Can you show me your clear arms, legs and body shape? Are you long and stretched or is there a body shape change somewhere?'

Lessons 2 and 3

Concentrate on the **'Where?'** of the movement, adding variety and quality by good use of own and whole floor space, directions and levels.

'Can you sometimes step on the spot, (particularly when you are in a crowded area) and sometimes use the whole room space – sides, corners, ends as well as middle.'

'Stepping actions sideways and backwards can be interesting – sliding, stepping-closing (chasse) or cross-stepping over, as well as feet passing normally. The leading leg can swing in many directions.'

Lessons 3 and 4

Consider the **'How?'** of the movements and the way that changes of speed and effort (force) might make the work look more controlled and neat, as well as giving them greater variety, contrast and interest.

'Within your stepping, can you include a change of speed? It might be slow, slow; quick, quick, 3, 4; slow, slow. Flat, flat; tip toes, tip toes, 3, 4; flat, flat.. This is interesting if a change of direction accompanies the speed change. Side, slow, slow; forward, quick, quick, 3, 4; side, slow, slow.' 'Can you make parts of your travelling small, soft, quiet, and make parts bigger, firmer, stronger?' (On the spot, keep it soft, 1, 2, 3, 4; on the move, big strong strides, 1, 2, 3, 4.)

Lessons 4 or Lessons 4 and 5

Ask for **sequences** that draw together all the practising, learning, adapting and remembering that have taken place during the previous lessons and aim for almost non-stop action, working harder for longer with enthusiasm, understanding and concentration.

'In your 3 or 4 part sequence, can you include: varied stepping actions, interesting use of space, and a change of speed or force somewhere?'

National Curriculum Requirements for Gymnastic Activities – Key Stage 1: The Main Features

'The government believes that two hours of physical activity a week, including the National Curriculum for Physical Education and extra-curricular activities, should be an aspiration for all schools. This applies to all stages.'

Programme of study

Pupils should be taught to:

a perform basic skills in travelling; being still; finding and using space both on the floor and using apparatus

b develop the range of their skills and actions (for example, balancing, jumping and landing, climbing, rolling)

c link skills and actions in short movement phrases

d create and perform short, linked sequences that show a clear beginning, middle and end with contrasts in direction, level and speed.

Attainment target

Pupils should be able to demonstrate that they can:

a select and use skills, actions and ideas appropriately, applying them with control and co-ordination

b copy, explore and remember skills, and link them in ways that suit the activities

c observe and talk about differences between their own and others' performances and use this understanding to improve their own performance.

Main NC headings when considering assessment of progression and expectation

Planning thoughtfully precedes the performance. Pupils think ahead to what their response will be, trying to 'see' the intended outcome. Evidence of satisfactory planning is seen in:

a sensible, safe judgements

b an obvious understanding of what was asked for

c good use of the movement elements that enhance and provide quality, variety and contrast.

Performing and improving performance is the main aim and evident as pupils:

a work hard, concentrating on the main features of the task

b practise to show safe, skilful, controlled activity

c demonstrate that they can remember and repeat the actions.

Linking actions together, with control, into 'sentences of movement' with a still start and finish and a flowing middle, provides a basis for progression, and is evident as pupils:

a work harder for longer

b work more confidently

c show greater use of the space, shape and effort elements that provide attractive variety and contrast in sequences.

Reflecting and making judgements is evident as pupils:

a describe the most important features of a demonstration

b suggest ways to improve

c self-evaluate and act upon their own reflections.

Reception Gymnastic Activities Programme

Pupils should be able to:

Autumn	Spring	Summer
1 Stand still; look at and listen to the teacher; respond quietly to instructions, particularly requests to 'Stop!'	**1** Respond whole-heartedly and quietly to simple tasks, working hard to improve.	**1** Respond readily, quietly and immediately to instructions.
2 Travel in a variety of ways, using feet – walking, running, jumping, skipping, galloping, hopping, bouncing, hopscotch.	**2** Practise, almost without stopping, until told to change to something else.	**2** Contribute unselfishly to the safe, quiet working environment.
3 Travel using hands and feet, slowly, with varied actions, shapes, directions and different parts leading.	**3** Use feet neatly, travelling in varied ways, sharing the limited space sensibly.	**3** Show pride and pleasure from achieving, having practised to improve.
4 Lift, carry, place apparatus safely and sensibly, working with others co-operatively.	**4** Travel slowly on hands and feet in varied ways, including 'bunny jumps' and cartwheels.	**4** Perform vigorously because 'It is good for our fitness.'
5 Be space-aware, sharing floor and apparatus sensibly and unselfishly with others.	**5** Take weight safely on hands by keeping arms straight and head forward.	**5** Travel on hands and feet, with neat actions, good shapes and use of space.
6 Be shape-aware, in stillness and when travelling.	**6** Be aware of body parts used, and good body shapes, in travelling and stillness.	**6** Practise to improve the basic skills of running, jumping, rolling, climbing, hanging, inverting and balancing.
7 Enjoy linking a series of actions together, smoothly.	**7** Perform simple rolls, curled up small, and 'log rolls', sideways, with straight body.	**7** Take body weight safely on hands with straight arms and head forward, as in 'bunny jumps' and cartwheels.
8 Enjoy moving vigorously, believing 'These lessons are good for you, fun, exciting.'	**8** Plan responses to simple tasks. 'Can you show me...?'	**8** Jump to land safely from low apparatus without jarring, by 'giving' in knees.
9 Demonstrate willingly, when asked, to help observers, and to have own achievements recognised and explained.	**9** Practise landing from low apparatus without jarring, and a 'squashy give' in knees and ankles.	**9** Perform simple, side-to-side rolls, curled or 'log' rolls with stretched body.
10 Plan and perform simple skills safely.	**10** Lift, carry and place apparatus in co-operation with others.	**10** Be body-shape aware – wide, long, curled, arched – still, balanced or travelling.
11 Observe simple actions being demonstrated and describe and learn from pleasing features.	**11** Co-operate and work sensibly with a partner.	**11** Understand 'Over, under, across, along, around' during apparatus work.
	12 Watch demonstrations and comment on good work seen. Copy some features.	**12** Take part in simple partner activities such as leading and following.
		13 Link a short series of simple actions, such as walk, run, jump and land.
		14 When linking actions smoothly together, show a still start and finish position.
		15 Watch demonstrations with interest and be able to pick out and comment on features that are pleasing and worth copying.

Lesson Plan 1 • 30 minutes
September

Emphasis on: *(a) creating a quiet, industrious atmosphere with good responses to instruction; (b) good use of feet in travelling and jumping, sharing the limited space safely; (c) co-operating with others to lift, carry and place the simple apparatus quietly, safely and sensibly.*

Floorwork
12 minutes

Legs

1   Walk, using all the floor space, going in and out of one another.

2   When I call 'Stop!', show me how quickly you can find a space, all by yourself, not near anyone else. 'Stop!'

3   Let your arms swing as you walk, visiting all parts of the room where you can see a space.

4   Change to quiet running now. Can you go to the corners, ends and sometimes the middle of the room?

5   When I call 'Stop!', show me your lovely, running body shape (illustrated), in your own space. 'Stop!'

Legs and Body

1   Stay where you are, in your good space, and show me a big jump up and a nice, squashy landing.

2   Push the floor hard with both feet and feel your ankles stretching.

3   Really swing up with both arms to help your big jump. Let both arms swing backwards, then forwards, and right above your head.

4   In your landing, can you let your knees bend for a nice, soft, squashy landing?

Apparatus Work
16 minutes

1   Walk all around the room, but do not touch the apparatus yet. You may go under, over, along or in and out of the pieces, but do not touch them.

2   When I call 'Stop!', stop on the nearest piece of apparatus and really stretch up high to the ceiling. 'Stop!'

3   Now jump off with a nice, squashy landing on the floor, and off you go, walking, running or skipping in and out again. Are you going to all parts of the room, keeping well away from the other children? 'Stop!'

4   You may go on to the apparatus with a step or a jump, then jump down again, with your nice, squashy, quiet landing. Move to a different piece of apparatus.

5   I am looking at the ways you travel between apparatus. Please show me your very best walking, running, skipping or even bouncing. I am looking for beautifully neat feet and legs as you travel.

6   Can you show me a nicely stretched body as you jump from your apparatus, and then your squashy landing?

Final Floor Activity
2 minutes

Can you show me a way or ways to travel to all parts of the room, going in and out of one another? (Look out for and comment on neat examples of walking, running, skipping, hopping, bouncing with feet apart or together and slipping sideways.)

Teaching notes and NC guidance
Development over 3–4 lessons

Floorwork

Legs

1 Young primary school pupils will all follow one another in an anti-clockwise circle unless taught to do otherwise. We want them to 'Walk on straight lines, not curving, not following others.'

2 This is an exercise in listening for and giving an instant response to an instruction, namely to 'Stop!' Be firm with non-responders because they are time-wasting, diminishing the amount of time for activity and the enjoyment of the lesson.

3 Pursue 'good' movement, even in something as natural as walking. Good posture and smart, brisk walking, with praise where it is deserved, sets a standard of hard-working, vigorous effort for this and subsequent lessons.

4 Good, quiet running is marked by a good lifting in heels, knees and arms. Once again, pupils will tend to circle anti-clockwise, and they must be reminded 'Run straight, all by yourself.'

5 The exercise in responding asks for an immediate stop and an inclined body in a good running position, one leg and arm forward.

Legs and Body

1 Ensure that all are well spaced for the jumping, away from other children and all the surrounding apparatus.

2 A teacher demonstration of the push from the balls of the feet and the stretch of the ankle joint is recommended.

3 A long, slow arm swing starts behind you and goes up to a full stretch above head. Many of our physical activities can be assisted by a preliminary swing of the arms.

4 A teacher demonstration of the meaning of 'nice, squashy landing' is recommended until members of the class themselves can be asked to show the 'give' in knees and ankles for the safe, soft finish.

Apparatus Work

1 Encourage brisk walking on the floor without touching any apparatus. A teacher demonstration will explain 'over; under; in and out.' 'Along' can be astride a bench, for example.

2 On 'Stop!' respond immediately on the nearest piece of apparatus. Be perfectly still, stretched tall with arms reaching up.

3 The careful jump off uses the correct, 'giving' landing practised in the floorwork. We now encourage greater variety in the methods of travelling around apparatus.

4 Apparatus is now to be used freely, on and off, non-stop.

5 Look out for, praise and demonstrate examples of good quality and variety in the travelling on the floor.

6 The firm, stretched body in flight contrasts with the soft, 'giving' body on landing.

Final Floor Activity

Ask them to show their 'favourite' way or ways to travel to all parts of the hall, performed beautifully.

Lesson Plan 2 • 30 minutes
October

Emphasis on: *(a) experiencing enjoyment and excitement through participation in varied physical activity; (b) enjoying the unselfish co-operation of everyone in sharing the floor and apparatus space; (c) practising and learning varied, well-controlled ways of travelling on feet and on hands and feet; (d) establishing the tradition of lifting, carrying, placing and using apparatus quietly, safely and sensibly.*

Floorwork
12 minutes

Legs

1   Walk and run, quietly, in and out of one another, and visit every part of the room.

2   Can you go to the sides, corners, ends and sometimes through the middle of the room?

3   When I call 'Stop!' show me a big, high jump and a squashy landing in a space all by yourself. 'Stop!' (Repeat.)

4   Now, show me some other way or ways that you can travel, using your feet only. (Look out for and comment on hopping, skipping, galloping, bouncing.)

Body

1   Can you run one or two steps into a space near you, jump up high and then do a squashy landing? Then stand up, look for another space, and off you go again.

2   Can you help your good landings by holding your arms out forward or sideways to help your balance?

3   Your squashy landings will be even quieter if you land on your toes and then let your knees bend a little bit.

Arms

1   Can you travel about the hall using hands and feet only?

2   Travel very slowly (not scampering) and help yourself by keeping away from all the others.

3   Keep your arms nice and straight as you move them, and point your fingers forward.

Apparatus Work
16 minutes

1   Walk all around the room without touching any apparatus. You can go under, over, across, in and out of, and around the pieces, but don't touch any yet.

2   Now change to your own favourite ways to travel on the floor, still not touching apparatus. You might jump across part of a mat; step over a bench; crawl under a plank; creep through a space in the climbing frame; or bounce along, astride a bench.

3   Now using your feet only, can you show me ways of getting on to, travelling along, and then coming off the apparatus? Remember 'Feet only. No hands!'

4   Change now to using your hands and feet to help you on to the apparatus, and travel across or along it.

5   I would be very pleased to see you come on to the apparatus using your hands strongly in some way. (Look out for and comment on twists, levers, pulls and bunny jumps.)

6   I would like to see you leave some pieces of apparatus with a nice, stretched jump and a soft, squashy landing on your mat.

Final Floor Activity
2 minutes

Follow me, all walking... jogging... skipping.... bouncing... hopping... and now anything you like.

Teaching notes and NC guidance
Development over 3–4 lessons

Floorwork

Legs

1 Running quietly is helped by feeling a lifting in your heels and knees. The noisy, flat-footed style often seen (and heard) is quickly improved by some demonstrations.

2 The teacher can join in and show 'I am visiting the corner... the side... the middle... now one end... not following anyone.' This shows what is wanted when travelling about, sharing a small space.

3 For the sake of a virtually unimpeded, full and busy lesson, the immediate response must become a tradition in this and all physical education lessons.

4 Variety; trying out and learning new skills; individuality; and extending the repertoire of the teacher and class, are all being pursued here.

Body

1 One or two steps only, so that the jumping and landing are the main things. Restrain those who run all around the room before doing their jump. Tell them to look for the next space to run to.

2 A teacher demonstration of the meaning of 'Straight arms helping the balanced landing' will illustrate this good point.

3 A demonstration with half the class watching the other half can include the challenge 'Look out for and tell me who is landing on their toes, with knees bending a little bit.'

Arms

1 Most will start crawling far too quickly for it to have any beneficial effects. Slow, careful travel on hands and feet, particularly on apparatus, is what we are looking for.

2 Ask them to 'Look out for and travel into good spaces again' to counter the usual massing in the centre of the floor.

3 Straight arms are strong, safe arms, particularly when we move on to inverting and supporting the whole body on hands alone.

Apparatus Work

1 While the class are walking, using floor only, the teacher can do any last minute adjustments to the apparatus placement.

2 Planning, using appropriate actions, is called for to negotiate each piece of apparatus.

3 Now there's the fun of going on to, moving along, and then coming off the apparatus, but only using feet at this stage. Mostly, they will be stepping or jumping on and off, non-stop. Encourage them not to queue – another important tradition to establish.

4 Using hands and feet enables them to travel everywhere, including on the climbing frames where they were not able to work using feet only.

5 When coming on to climbing frames, demonstrate the correct, safe, 'fingers over, thumbs under' position. When weight is all on hands, ask for straight, strong arms, as when coming on to or crossing a bench.

6 While hands are important in helping you onto apparatus, the feet will be important in helping you off. The jumps off are exhilarating to young pupils, and we want them to be safe in their landings.

Lesson Plan 3 • 30 minutes
November

Emphasis on: *(a) planning and performing simple skills safely; (b) body-shape awareness, both in held positions, such as a balance, and in travelling; and in working hard to show a neat, firm body shape to enhance the look of the work.*

Floorwork
12 minutes

Legs

1 Can you run and jump up high to show me different body shapes in the air?

2 A long, stretched shape like a pencil looks very lively.

3 A big star shape with arms and legs stretched wide is a very neat, strong shape to try.

4 What other shapes are there? (Look out for and comment on twists and tucks with knees bent.)

Body

1 Can you stand, balanced tall on tiptoes? It sometimes helps if you put one foot in front of the other. Stretch your arms out in front of you or to one side to help balance.

2 Slowly, can you lift one foot off the floor a little way and show me a new balance on just one foot? What strong body shape are you using to hold you nice and still?

3 Now, can you lower down to sitting and roll back on to your shoulders to balance in a small, curled up shape?

4 Roll forwards again, up to standing tall and stretched on tiptoes. Let's start all over again.

Arms

1 As you travel slowly, using hands and feet, can you show me a long shape, a wide shape or a small, curled shape?

2 Can you be very clever and go from a curled to a new shape as you travel carefully from space to space?

3 Travelling with straight arms and legs is very difficult but strong. Can anyone show me travelling where your body parts are strong and straight?

Apparatus Work
16 minutes

1 Run around the room without touching any apparatus. I hope that you are lifting your heels and your knees to keep your running quiet and make it look good.

2 When I call 'Stop!' show me a clear body shape on the nearest piece of apparatus. Make your body long, wide, curled, twisted or arched like a bridge. 'Stop!' (Repeat.)

3 Now you can go on to all the apparatus. Try to find places where you can show me different body shapes. (For example, stretched hanging on a rope; standing wide on the climbing frame; curled up on a mat; arched across a box top.)

4 Remember some of the ways you travelled on hands and feet on the floor. Can you do some of these actions, slowly and carefully, using the apparatus?

5 Finally, you are going to travel on the apparatus and hold a balance somewhere. Then do a nice, stretched jump up and off the apparatus, followed by a beautiful, squashy landing.

Final Floor Activity
2 minutes

After a short run, show me a jump upwards with arms and legs stretched long or wide like a pencil or a star.

Teaching notes and NC guidance
Development over 4 lessons

Floorwork

Legs

1   'Can you...?' or 'Show me....' are expressions repeatedly used to give pupils a new challenge.

2   A teacher demonstration can be done in a standing position or, better still, moving, to show a very short run-up of two or three steps only.

3   The star is difficult because pupils have to jump high enough to give time for the feet to come together before landing.

4   If there are no suggestions, let the class all stand and feel a twist of one body part against another; or a tuck that can be practised in the crouch position with knees bent; or a bridge shape bent forwards, sideways or high backwards.

Body

1   All follow the teacher in to the tiptoes balance and hold it. Wobbling is lessened by stretching arms to front or sides.

2   Lift one foot a very small way if the balance is difficult. To help, the whole body can counterbalance by leaning slightly the other way.

3   The slow lower to sitting; the roll back on to shoulders; and the curled balance on shoulders should not be a problem if the back is kept rounded for the roll, with chin on chest.

4   One long down-and-up swing from shoulder balance to standing, pretending someone is pulling you.

Arms

1   Much of the travelling will be crawling to start with. This can be developed by crawling on hands and knees, then on hands and feet, which means going from curled to stretched. Hands and feet can be close together, giving a long, narrow shape, or spread wide apart.

2   The transfer from curled to stretched can be performed with front, back or side towards the floor, travelling on hands only, then on feet only.

3   Travelling on straight arms and legs can be a normal crawling action or one where hands only travel first, then feet only. The body moves from a long, low position to a high hips position.

Apparatus Work

1   'Good running' is not common and continually needs to be asked for, explained and demonstrated.

2   If the running has been well spaced out, the balances on apparatus should be equally well spaced out and unimpeded. Good examples of wobble-free, firm, hard-working balances should be commented on, praised and demonstrated.

3   Pupils go from apparatus to apparatus, holding a still position with an obvious shape being the challenge. They can be on, under, along, across or angled against the apparatus.

4   To increase the repertoire of the class and teacher, half the class at a time can demonstrate a range of actions to the others using hands and feet for travelling on apparatus.

5   Travelling on floor on feet, and on hands and feet; on all apparatus using hands and feet; held balances on apparatus; and the jump up and from apparatus, provide an exciting variety.

Final Floor Activity

All running together to one end of the room, jump up and stretch; all back to opposite end, jump high in a star.

Lesson Plan 4 • 30 minutes
December

Emphasis on: *(a) awareness of space, and of where you and others are going as you share the floor and the apparatus; (b) a caring attitude towards yourself and others as you move vigorously but safely on floor and apparatus; (c) working and practising hard to improve and enjoy the linking together of a series of actions.*

Floorwork
12 minutes

Legs

1   Can you travel around the room on your feet, sometimes forwards, sometimes sideways?

2   What actions are good for going forwards? (For example, walking, running, skipping or hopping.)

3   What actions help you to travel sideways the best? (For example, walking, with small steps or lively skipping; feet together bouncing; galloping.)

Body

1   Show me a favourite, still balance, reaching high with both arms. No wobbling!

2   Can you now reach out to the space in front of you or to one side of you, still balancing without wobbling?

3   Can you choose a different part of your body now to balance on, reaching out to a low position to steady you? (The above sequence could include going from standing tall to leaning forwards on one foot, to crouching on hands and knees. Accompany each action with a reaching out to a different point in the surrounding space.)

Arms

1   With all your weight on your hands, can you lift your feet up from the floor and put them down in a different place?

2   Keep your arms straight for a strong position, and make your fingers point forwards.

3   You can lift your feet from side to side over the lines on the floor. You can jump them in between or outside your hands, perhaps twisting as you go.

Apparatus Work
16 minutes

1   Can you travel up to, along and from a piece of apparatus, and show me a change of direction?

2   Remember that your travelling is on both floor and apparatus. What neat ways are you using to travel on feet, or on hands and feet?

3   A change of direction means that the side of your body or your back starts to lead the action, rather than the front of your body, as when you are going forwards.

4   Be careful when you go backwards. Look to see that you have plenty of space before stepping or jumping backwards.

5   Show me travelling where you are low or near to the floor or apparatus. (For example, pulling along a bench; sliding down a plank; rolling on a mat; climbing, near to the frame; crawling under a plank.)

6   Use your feet only to travel up to and on to each piece of apparatus. Now show me a still, beautifully stretched balance high above the apparatus. Then jump down with a nice, squashy landing, and travel to the next piece of apparatus.

Final Floor Activity
2 minutes

Can you run and jump to land facing in a new direction?

Teaching notes and NC guidance
Development over 4 lessons

Floorwork

Legs

1 As the teacher says the words 'forwards' and 'sideways', he or she can show the meanings by moving forwards, then sideways.

2 Emphasise 'forwards' actions for a minute or two, giving examples if the class needs guidance.

3 A similar emphasis as above, but on 'sideways' this time. Explain that the side of your body leads when you are travelling sideways.

Body

1 'Balance' means that your body is supported by some unusual body part or apparatus surface and feels unsteady. We have to work hard not to wobble about. The reaching out here is to a *high* level.

2 The reaching out here is to a *medium* level.

3 The reaching out here is to a *low* level. These three levels are in our own surrounding air space. Levels, like directions and our own and general space, can be used to give greater interest, variety and contrast to gymnastic activities.

Arms

1 The pupils are being given practice in 'feeling' where their feet are on the floor space that surrounds them. Strong arm and shoulder exercise accompanies this activity.

2 This strong exercise is performed most effectively by keeping both arms straight, with fingers pointing forwards as normal. Bent arms are in a weak position; fingers and hands pointing outwards do not work efficiently or safely.

3 Suggestions from the teacher are necessary to develop this unusual activity of lifting feet from the floor and placing them down in a 'new place'. Good, safe ideas and ways to perform this on the floor will be helpful later, when the same action is performed on apparatus.

Apparatus Work

1 The change of direction can be performed anywhere – after rope swing; coming from bench or low box; as pupil walks along a plank; on floor between pieces of apparatus; after landing from a jump.

2 Teacher commentary can enthuse about the many travelling actions being seen. Neat climbing, swinging, rolling, running and jumping, circling, skipping, bouncing, etc.

3 Give pupils a reminder that they have to plan a direction change within their travelling up to, on to, along and from the apparatus.

4 It is helpful to stop the whole class and ask them to stand on a low piece of apparatus or a mat. 'Very carefully now, look behind you. If there is no-one in the way, step or jump off backwards to land softly and nicely balanced. Ready? Go!'

5 Low-level travelling means being near to the floor and apparatus, gripping strongly to pull, circle, climb, slide, roll in close proximity to floor and apparatus.

6 A high-level stretch in contrast to the previous activity will take pupils away from the apparatus.

Final Floor Activity

Landing to face a new direction is often necessary anyway when your run and jump takes you near to a wall.

Lesson Plan 5 • 30 minutes
January

Gymnastic Activities

Emphasis on: *(a) travelling, and experiencing the many ways that our feet, hands and large body surfaces can support and carry us; (b) an awareness of the many actions and uses of body parts that are possible as we travel.*

Floorwork
12 minutes

Legs

1   Can you walk, then run, jump and start running again, without stopping?

2   Because you are travelling without stopping, plan to make your walk and run short enough to give you plenty of room to do your lively jump and its landing, followed straight away by your next set of walking. No stopping!

3   Travel along straight lines, never following anyone. Always look for good spaces in the room.

Body

1   Travel by going from stretched to curled body, using different body parts to support you.

2   Can you lie on your back, stretched out; then curl up tight, holding your hands together under your knees; roll over on to one side; then stretch out long again?

3   From standing tall and stretched up high, can you lower slowly down to a curled sitting position? If you are very clever, you might rock back, still curled up small, then stretch up while balancing on your shoulders.

Arms

1   Start in a curled, crouched position on hands and feet. Can you move your hands only until your body is long and stretched, then move your feet forwards again to your curled, start position?

2   Do this very slowly so that your body is working hard. You can do it with feet and hands close together or wide apart. Which way feels harder to do?

3   Can anyone show me another slow way to travel using feet and hands? (Demonstrate a selection of 'other ways' to help them remember.)

Apparatus Work
16 minutes

1   Travel without stopping to all parts of the room, without touching apparatus. Can you do your floorwork walking, running, jumping without stopping? (For example, walking across, under, through apparatus, running on floor, across mats, astride benches; jumping over mats, benches.)

2   Use your feet only now to bring you on to, take you along and bring you off the apparatus. Plan to show me a good variety of actions. (For example, step, jump or bounce on; walk, skip, bounce, run, hop, balance along; step, jump and swing up and off.)

3   Now travel slowly, using hands and feet, up to, on, along and from each piece of apparatus in turn. Travel slowly so that I can easily see your strong, neat actions.

4   On floor and apparatus, can you travel by changing from a long, stretched shape to a round, curled shape? Your curled shape can take you into a roll to travel to your next stretch.

5   You can stretch and curl your way across the climbing frame; on and under planks, poles and benches; and rolling across mats.

Final Floor Activity
2 minutes

Show me a way to travel silently using your feet.

Teaching notes and NC guidance
Development over 4 lessons

Floorwork

Legs

1 Three or four walking steps followed by four or five running steps provide a nice, reasonably short rhythm before the 'Jump and start walking again.'

2 The lively jump will be done with full swing up of the arms. This arm action, plus a 'give' of the knees and ankles on landing, helps to balance and control you as you land.

3 With young primary school pupils we continually have to ask them not to circulate in a curving, anti-clockwise direction. By moving in a straight line, they will seldom be following anyone, and the direction changes needed as they come to the outside take them to all parts of the room.

Body

1 To help them to get the idea and get started, we can show pupils a crouch position, on feet only, curled down near the floor. Then we can take them into a big stretch up and step forwards, one foot after the other, to standing tall.

2 Alternating whole body stretches and curls is most easily done while lying down with front, back or side towards the floor.

3 This little sequence takes pupils from a high to a lower level as well as from a stretch to a curl, and includes lowering and rolling as linking movements.

Arms

1 Emphasise straight arms for a safe, strong position, particularly if there is a moment when the hands take all the body weight as the feet are jumped forwards.

2 If the legs as well as the arms are kept straight, a high, arched dome shape alternates with the long, low, straight shape.

3 Pupils can travel with back towards floor; with feet or one side leading rather than head; with bunny jumps or cartwheels.

Apparatus Work

1 Planning to walk, then run, then jump somewhere and carry on walking without stopping gives pupils a good challenge.

2 Thoughtful travelling on feet only calls for well-controlled steps, jumps and bounces, and good, safe, sensible landing actions.

3 A wide variety of ways to grip, hold and support yourself on, around, across and under the apparatus are practised here.

4 'Hands only first. Feet only next.' Crouch to stretch to crouch is the simplest way to alternate between these two shapes. This is done easily on mats, benches, boxes, planks and on one side of the climbing frame.

5 Stand, roll, stand; lie straight, curl, lie straight; bring hands and feet close together, then take them apart on floor, on top of and under surfaces; or swing on a rope with a curled body and land with a straight body. These are all ways to answer this task.

Final Floor Activity

The teacher can say 'While you are travelling, using your feet silently, I will keep my eyes closed. I don't want to hear a sound. Can you make me think no-one is moving?'

Lesson Plan 6 • 30 minutes
February

Gymnastic Activities

Emphasis on: *(a) planning and performing basic actions, including jumping and landing, rolling and taking weight on hands; (b) showing concern for self and others by good behaviour and sensible sharing of space.*

Floorwork
12 minutes

Legs

1 Can you do some little bouncing jumps in your own space, then run to a space near you and do another jump?

2 The bouncing jumps will be quiet if you push off with your toes and let your knees and ankles bend softly on landing.

3 Can you land from your running jump and be still, without any wobbling about? Arms that stretch out in front can help you to land and balance nicely.

Body

1 Can you sit down with your back rounded and your head down on your knees? Now try to rock backwards and forwards, with your body rolling like a ball, all the way from your seat to your shoulders. Backwards and forwards; backwards and forwards.

2 Now can you lie on your back with your hands clasped together under your knees, making your body round and small? Try a little rock from side to side now.

3 Can you join up for me a little rock backwards and forwards, then side to side? Keep your back curled and head forward on knees, just like a rolling ball.

Arms

1 Stand and hold your hands in front towards me. Keep the arms straight. Bend down and put your hands on the floor. Can you push on your hands, and jump your feet up off the floor?

2 We call this 'bunny jumping'. Keep your head looking forwards, with arms strong and straight.

3 Keep your legs bent, and push feet hard against the floor.

4 Keep your hands pointing forwards and your fingers spread.

Apparatus Work
16 minutes

1 At all low pieces of apparatus, use your feet only to bring you on to the apparatus. (For example, step, jump, bounce or run on to benches, barbox top, barbox bottom, planks or mats.)

2 Jump down from your low apparatus on to the mat, and show me a beautifully soft, squashy landing, which can take you down slowly on to your back. Then do a little roll sideways right over on to your front. Jump up, and off you go again!

3 Once again, hold your arms out towards me showing me straight arms. Walk around, putting both hands on each piece of apparatus, and jump your feet off the floor. Head looks forward.

4 As you come towards each piece of apparatus, can you do a little upwards jump on the spot, then walk, jog or run up to the apparatus and carefully take your weight on your hands?

5 Walk around now, visiting each of the mats, and have a little go at your rocking and rolling movements that we practised in the floorwork. Sit down, see that you have room and then practise forwards and backwards, or side to side.

Final Floor Activity
2 minutes

Can you do sets of four jumps, turning to face a different side of the room each time?

Teaching notes and NC guidance
Development over 4 lessons

Floorwork

Legs

1   The main features of jumping or bouncing on the spot are a good stretch of the ankle joint and a push off from the balls of the feet. One or two good demonstrators will give the class a picture of what is wanted.

2   The knees, ankles and hips all 'give' like springs on landing. This 'giving', cushioned, recoiled landing is particularly important when landing safely from a height.

3   The jump after the run will be a forwards one, contrasting with the starting jump upwards. To help balance a forwards jump, hold straight arms out in front at shoulder height.

Body

1   If the class mirror the teacher, who sits down at the front with knees bent, back rounded, chin down on chest, they will be in a good position straight away.

2   A swing to the side by the knees takes you sideways. Demonstrate with a good example the importance of the well-rounded back for easy rocking.

3   'Backwards and forwards; one side, the other side; to shoulders, to seat; to left and to right.'

Arms

1   All stand facing teacher, holding both arms straight out to show the straight-arm position, fingers pointing forwards. This is the basis for a strong, safe, ungiving arm position when all the body weight is on the hands only.

2   If the head looks backwards under the arms instead of forwards, everything will be upside down and the pupils will be disorientated. 'Look forwards to see everything normally.'

3   Bent legs are short levers, which can be lifted quickly.

4   We need to remind pupils to place both hands strongly facing forwards, not out to the sides.

Apparatus Work

1   We focused on the importance of hands in the previous activity on the floor. Now we are focusing on the feet and the many varied, neat actions that they can perform at apparatus.

2   A jump down that flows slowly and carefully into a squashy landing on the mat is an enjoyable sequence – the firm, straight, vigorous jump from apparatus contrasting with a soft, easy, curled roll down at a low level.

3   With straight arms, pupils now visit each piece of apparatus and perform a little bunny jump, momentarily taking all their weight on the hands only. 'Straight arms and bent legs, and keep looking forwards.'

4   A little jump on the spot before travelling, as practised at the start of the floorwork, gives an added momentum to the bunny jumps on the apparatus, making them easier.

5   The ten or so mats in a well-provided hall provide ample opportunities for practising the favourite rolling action in comfort. Moving around until you see a quiet space on a mat is also an exercise in 'showing concern for self and others.'

Final Floor Activity

All can face the front, then the side being pointed to by the teacher, then the back, then the other side, then back to the front again, enjoying working together in unison.

Year R

Lesson Plan 7 • 30 minutes
March

Emphasis on: *(a) partner work to provide new experiences and develop desirable social relationships; (b) being interested in and able to observe simple actions, and to copy, describe and learn from pleasing features.*

Floorwork
12 minutes

Legs

1 From a still starting position, one partner performs a short travel, a jump and landing, and a still, balanced finish. The other partner observes and copies.

2 Can you improve your sequence by showing a good body shape at the beginning, in your jump, and at the end?

3 Watching partner, did you see how many feet your partner jumped from? Was it one or both?

4 Are you landing with feet together or apart, or even with one foot after the other?

Body and arms

1 One partner makes a shape like a bridge, supported on hands and feet. The other partner travels underneath, over, across, through, and in and out of this bridge shape, without touching the still partner (illustrated).

2 Change places and repeat the activity. The new bridge-making partner can be on hands and feet, or some other parts of the body, for support. Can the travelling partner go under, across, through or in and out of this new bridge without touching it?

3 Keep on practising in your own time, making a still, strong bridge, then travelling, one after the other.

4 If you are taking a lot of weight on your hands when making a bridge or travelling under or over, remember to keep your arms straight for a safe, strong support.

Apparatus Work
16 minutes

1 Follow your leader up to and on to each piece of apparatus, and show me a beautifully clear body shape in a still, balanced position. One after the other, leave your apparatus, travel to the next piece and show me another still balance with a clear body shape.

2 As you travel on the floor between apparatus, are you trying to copy your partner's travelling actions? If I asked you to show me, would you be doing the same thing?

3 The other partner will lead now. Can you show me some travelling, both on floor and apparatus, where you use your arms strongly? (This can include hands only and a bunny jump on apparatus and floor.)

4 It helps if the leader goes first, travels a little distance and then waits for the partner (who has stood still, watching very carefully) to follow.

Final Floor Activity
2 minutes

Take turns at follow-the-leader and show your following partner your favourite way or ways to travel neatly and quietly using your feet, e.g. walking, running, jumping, skipping, hopping, bouncing, slipping sideways, hopscotch.

Teaching notes and NC guidance
Development over 4 lessons

Floorwork

Legs

1 It helps if a couple chooses and stays in a small area of the room, free from the distraction of other couples, and works backwards and forwards on their own private 'stage'. The alternative is usually a circle of pairs getting in each others' way as they push up against the couple in front.

2 A good body shape means you are working hard (no lazy sagging); improving the appearance of the performance; and showing good body control, one of several reasons why we do Physical Education.

3 The usual one-footed take-off is best for a long jump. The less common two-footed take-off is best for an upwards, high jump.

4 Landing with one foot after the other helps to slow you down gradually for a more controlled finish. However, landing on two feet is the usual method practised.

Body and arms

1 If the pupils are asked, 'Can anyone point out a bridge-like shape in the room?' someone will point to a trestle, the outline of the barbox, or the side walls and ceiling of the room. This gives them a picture of the arched shapes we are looking for.

2 The front, back or one side of the body can be facing the floor. The bridge can be on hands and knees; hands and feet; under knees while seated; under knees while lying; under front, back or side of body while the bridge-maker is standing with body arched.

3 Pointing out examples of different level bridges – high on feet only; medium on hands and feet only; low lying on back or front with a shallow bridge – extends the class repertoire and the ways of negotiating that can be experimented with.

4 With back or front to the floor, and on hands and feet only, it is important to keep the arms firm and straight. It is also good exercise for parts of the body seldom exercised strongly.

Apparatus Work

1 If they follow the leader at a distance of 2–3 metres, they will be able to observe and copy the actions; the exact use of the body parts concerned; and the body shapes used in the travelling. For the 'clear body shape in a still balance' on apparatus, the leader will need to wait for the follower to join him or her on the apparatus and hold still for two or three seconds as a pair.

2 A demonstration by a good leading and following couple, moving almost as one, is recommended. Half of the class at a time can be asked to show their still balances to identify the many supporting body parts possible. The majority will be on feet only. We want balances on seat; shoulders; one hand and one foot; tummy across plank or bench; one foot only, etc.

3 'Using your arms strongly when travelling, make full use now of all the apparatus, being sensible to ensure that there is enough room for you and your partner.'

4 'Leader, travel a short distance, then stop and wait for your partner to copy you and catch up.' This will break the activity down into: (a) the travel on the floor; (b) the mount and travel along the apparatus; and (c) the dismount and leaving the apparatus. A neat, tall, still position at start and finish each time enhances the impression and the appearance enormously.

Final Floor Activity

Each can lead two or three times, giving time for seeing, copying and mirroring exactly.

Lesson Plan 8 • 30 minutes
April

Emphasis on: *(a) planning and practising to link two or three actions together; (b) demonstrating greater confidence through neat, controlled work.*

Floorwork
12 minutes

Legs

1 Can you do an upwards jump where you are, then show me a very short run and another high jump?

2 In each jump, can you stretch your whole body beautifully?

3 When you land, can you let your knees and ankles 'give' softly and quietly?

Body

1 Show me a favourite, still body shape. (Stretched, arched, wide, curled, twisted or bridge-like.)

2 Can you move on to a different part of your body and show me a new body shape?

3 Try to make up a little sequence of three joined-up and different body shapes that you can remember and repeat.

Arms

1 Bend your knees, crouch down and put your hands flat on the floor just in front of you. Your weight is now supported on your hands and feet.

2 Can you show me two or three ways to lift your feet off the floor and then put them down quietly in a different place?

3 You can lift them and put them down on the same spot; or twist to one side; or lift the feet to go forwards, outside or between your hands.

Apparatus Work
16 minutes

1 Stand tall on tiptoes, showing me a beautifully still, stretched body shape. Now travel up to and on to a piece of apparatus and show me a still, firm body shape. Leave your first piece of

apparatus, travel and stop in a new floor space, once again showing me your beautifully stretched body. (Repeat up to and on to the next piece of apparatus.)

2 From your own floor space, can you make your hands important as you travel up to, on to, along and from each piece of apparatus, in turn? Finish back in your own space on the floor.

3 Keep both arms straight and strong as you put hands only on the apparatus. Lift bent legs off the floor to take all the weight on your hands (illustrated). You can put your feet down on the same spot or a new one (e.g. to cross a bench).

4 Stay at the piece of apparatus where you are now. Can you be very clever and join together for me: (a) a still, stretched, balanced starting position; (b) your way of travelling up to and on to the apparatus, using feet only or both feet and hands; (c) a still position on the apparatus with a clear body shape; (d) a neat, still finishing position, away from the apparatus, on the floor?

Final Floor Activity
2 minutes

Can you run and jump high, then run and jump long?

Teaching notes and NC guidance
Development over 4 lessons

Floorwork

Legs

1 A very short run of two or three strides only will take pupils to a nearby space for the second jump. They should almost feel and hear their rhythm: 'Jump; run, run, run and jump.'

2 The stretch while in the air should extend from the top of the head right down to the pointed toes. This is neat, looks good and 'correct', and makes the work more demanding and physical.

3 The 'squashy' landing makes this, and landings from a greater height, quiet and safe.

Body

1 For a quick start, everyone can do a standing, tall, stretched body shape, mirroring the teacher. Emphasise the firm feeling, with no lazy, sagging parts, and the complete stillness in position.

2 If help is needed to move pupils on to their next and different position and shape, the teacher can offer, 'Your seat; your knees; your shoulders; on to one foot only; your back, front or side; one hand and one foot.'

3 If a demonstration is arranged, the class can be asked to look out for 'Which body parts were supported? What shapes did you see? What movements were used to link them together?'

Arms

1 Flat hands pointing forwards, about shoulder width apart, and the arms kept straight. These important points for a safe, strong support can be taught as a whole class activity first.

2 The perfect position for a bunny jump has shoulders above hips above hands. Bent legs lift more easily than straighter ones.

3 One landing on the same spot; one that twists to one side or over a line; one where you reach forwards on to hands (in a new floor space) and pull legs up to a new place. These provide a good mixture.

Apparatus Work

1 We are aiming to develop a pattern that will apply in nearly all apparatus work henceforth, namely: (a) a still, ready starting position in own floor space; (b) a travel up to and on to the apparatus; (c) an activity that pupils have been challenged to do while on the apparatus; (d) a coming away from the apparatus to finish; (e) tall and still, in a floor space.

2 On ropes, climbing frames, trestles, planks and poles, benches and barboxes, hand activity is important. The class are being made aware of the many ways that we grip, support, pull, hang, climb, circle or twist across the varied pieces of apparatus.

3 Fingers should point forwards with arms strong and straight. Head looks forwards, not back under the arms, so that we see things the right way up, not upside down. Bent legs are short levers that make the lift up off the floor easier. Along with the guidance to keep 'fingers over and thumbs under' when gripping the bars of the climbing frame, this is a most important safety guidance.

4 Ask them to keep their little sequences 'little' as they plan to include the five elements requested. Proud, confident, still starting and finishing positions can be praised and shown.

Final Floor Activity

A short run to make the jumps the main part.

 **Year R**

Lesson Plan 9 • 30 minutes
May

Emphasis on: *(a) experiencing the use of different degrees of speed and force to contribute variety and contrast to performances; (b) enthusiastic participation in physical activity and believing that these lessons are fun, good for you and exciting.*

Floorwork
12 minutes

Legs

1 Can you walk forwards very slowly on tiptoes and, when you see an empty space near you, run, speeding up, and show me an explosive high jump?

2 Be still every time before you start. Still; then slow walk; then speed up and explode!

3 Can you feel nice and loose as you walk, and feel strong as you run and jump?

Body

1 Can you show me a balance with part of your body firm and stretched? (For example: on tiptoes with arms stretched; on one foot with non-supporting leg stretched; seated with arms and legs stretched; on shoulders with both legs stretched.)

2 Can you relax and gently move on to another part or parts to balance strongly again, stretching parts of your body? (Linking movements are rolls, lowers, twists.)

3 Keep going and try to do two or three, all nicely linked.

4 Can you 'feel' the difference between the strong stretches and the easy, relaxed way you change between them?

Arms

1 Pretend you are a kicking horse as you take all your weight on both hands and kick your feet backwards and forwards in the air. Make the kicks strong and fast, like the rear legs of a horse.

2 Horses, can you come back down to the floor with very gentle and quiet feet?

3 Keep your arms long and straight for a strong position, and look fowards with your head, not back under the arms which makes everything appear upside down.

Apparatus Work
16 minutes

1 Show me a mixture of slow, relaxed travelling away from apparatus (e.g. walking, easy jogging, skipping) with hardly a sound from anyone. Remember to visit all parts of the room: sides, ends, corners and the middle.

2 Show me a strong action as you work near the apparatus, still without touching it (e.g. run and jump over parts of mats; bounce along astride benches; swing into high jump across a low plank.)

3 Using all the apparatus now, can you get on to it using hands strongly, and travel using hands and feet?

4 Start on the floor near the apparatus and show me a balance on tiptoes or on one foot only, with a part of your body stretched strongly. Relax and travel up to the apparatus to show me a new balance, not on feet only, with a part of your body stretched strongly.

5 Can you show me a lively, vigorous jump from low apparatus, then a soft, squashy landing and an easy, relaxed roll sideways on your mat?

Final Floor Activity
2 minutes

Do some soft, slow, quiet jumps on the spot, then run into a speeding-up high jump.

Gymnastic Activities

Teaching notes and NC guidance
Development over 4 lessons

Floorwork

Legs

1 Emphasise that it is a very short run only into the explosive high jump. Some pupils will run all around the room with very few jumps being practised. They can be asked to 'Walk... now stop! Can you point to a good space very near you? Get ready to run two or three steps, speeding up into your high jump... Go!'

2 The interesting contrasts here are: stillness; slow motion; acceleration; stillness.

3 The class can be asked, 'Does your body feel different when you walk and when you speed up for your jump?' to describe changes in body tension.

Body

1 Explain that 'balance' means being on some small or unusual part or parts of your body and not wobbling, although you feel unsteady.

2 The parts being stretched are those parts not being used to support you.

3 A simple trio could include: standing; lower to sitting; roll back to shoulder balance.

4 The strong, hard working, unsagging stretch contrasts with the easy, giving, relaxed linking movements.

Arms

1 Kicking while on the hands is easier than trying to hold a handstand balance with feet together. The rapid leg movements seem to help the balancing.

2 Legs bend from the straight kicking to come down gently to the floor.

3 Straight arms, and hands at shoulder width pointing forwards, are the main teaching points.

Apparatus Work

1 The planning requested here is for easy, soft, slow action and a good use of all the space for the sake of self and others.

2 Greater effort is now called for to negotiate apparatus, still without touching it.

3 Strong hand positions include the thumbs-under grip on bars; hands together when swinging on a rope; gripping at sides of bench, planks and low barbox; and the straight arms on flat surfaces as you vault or bunny jump across.

4 A pattern of: a firm, still, stretched balance; a relaxed, easy travel; and a firm, still, stretched balance.

5 The contrast between the strong, stretched, explosive leap up and off to a high level, and the gentle, relaxed, rounded roll at low level, makes for an attractive and varied performance.

Final Floor Activity

Soft, almost slow-motion jumping on the spot needs a full bend and stretch in the ankle and knee joints, and a good, high action. In the speeding-up run, pupils can pretend to be springing up and on to a bench.

Lesson Plan 10 • 30 minutes
June

Emphasis on: *(a) partner work, because it is good fun and interesting, and lets you perform new activities you cannot do on your own; (b) watching another and answering questions on what was seen and liked.*

Floorwork
12 minutes

Legs

1 Follow your leader, who will show you two or three different actions to copy, using legs only.

2 Keep about two steps behind your leader so that you can see what his or her feet are doing.

3 Leader, if it is crowded, do an action on the spot.

Body

1 The new leader will demonstrate a nice, clear body shape for the partner to copy. You can be stretched long; curled like a ball (illustrated); wide like a star; arched like a bridge; or twisted.

2 The same leader now changes slowly to a new, clear body shape, and might need to do it on a new part of the body. Partner watches and copies. (For example, a smooth change from a high stretch, standing, down to a curled crouch, still on both feet.)

3 Leader, can you show your partner and me a third and last new body shape, please? (For example, a smooth change from a crouch to a bridge-like shape, standing, with upper body arched forwards, arms pointing down to floor.)

Arms

1 Travel side by side, moving hands only, then feet only. Try to move in unison.

2 Two of you need a lot of room. Move towards the best space you can see.

3 Are you moving with hands and feet close together or wide apart? Remember to keep your arms straight for a strong support.

Apparatus Work
16 minutes

1 Follow your leader in and out of all the apparatus, without touching any yet. Can you travel on straight lines, not following anyone else? I would like to see two or three travelling actions.

2 Now the other partner will lead as you travel up to each piece of apparatus, on to or across it for a very short time, then away from it. (No long travels or lingering on apparatus.)

3 Can you start at opposite sides or ends of a piece of apparatus and travel to cross to your partner's side? (Both may move at same time, space permitting, on climbing frames or mats, across barbox or plank. On narrow apparatus, one may need to cross first before the second moves.)

4 As you cross the apparatus this time, can you stop for a moment to show your partner and me a whole body shape that you like to make somewhere on the apparatus?

Final Floor Activity
2 minutes

Stand facing each other. Now jump up and down quietly, with a good stretch in your ankles. Can you be very clever and bounce together at the same time?

Teaching notes and NC guidance
Development over 4 lessons

Floorwork

Legs

1 Teacher commentary on actions observed will help to inspire a more varied response. 'I see good stepping, running, hopping, bouncing, jumping, hopscotch, skipping and slipping.' (A quick demonstration of neat, well-controlled, varied activities will be productive.)

2 When observing actions we look out for: the action itself; the way that body parts are working; any interesting shapes that are being used. (For example, skipping, with high knees and arms well lifted, and bent legs and straight arms.)

3 'On the spot, then moving' is always an interesting and varied use of floor space and worth encouraging.

Body

1 Early in the lesson's development it is a good idea to suggest doing this while on one or both feet. All the shapes possible can be shown while on the feet, and it gets everything moving quickly.

2 A very slow change from shape to shape will enable the following partner to do it at the same time, saving waiting and watching time, and leading to more action.

3 'Good things happen in threes.' A sequence with three parts is short enough to be remembered, but long enough to be varied and interesting.

Arms

1 Very slow travel on hands and then feet means that the body is working hard to support itself, and that both partners can work in unison, which is particularly pleasurable.

2 When travelling on hands and feet, young pupils often tend to move in towards the centre of the room. Encourage travelling out to the extremities where there is more space.

3 Hands and feet close together makes a high arch. When hands and feet are apart after the hands alone have gone forwards, the low arch position created is hard to hold.

Apparatus Work

1 Demonstrate with two or three couples, whose spacing and choice of neat and varied actions is admirable.

2 A 'quick on and off the apparatus' suggests jumps over; bunny jumps across; twists across; short swing on rope; or a roll across a mat.

3 From facing each other on opposite sides, travel a short way up to, on to, along, around or across the apparatus; then a short distance to partner's starting place on the floor.

4 Let pupils repeat it two or three times where they are, then demonstrations by half of the class at a time. This shows them good ideas to use when they change around to work at a new piece of apparatus.

Final Floor Activity

Slow, quiet jumps need a good, high lift from a strong stretch of the ankles, followed by a soft 'give' in knees, ankles and hips on landing.

Lesson Plan 11 • 30 minutes
July

Emphasis on: *(a) planning and performing short, simple sequences of two or three movements linked together to produce a pleasing performance; (b) reflecting that pupils have looked forward to and enjoyed taking part in vigorous action in these lessons during the past year.*

Floorwork
12 minutes

Legs

1 Show me two ways to walk, run, jump and land, including a still start and finish each time.

2 What body shape are you holding at start and finish, and in your jump? Make it clear.

3 What actions are you using as you take off and land?

Body

1 Change from being curled up small to a different body shape. Then change back again to being tightly curled.

2 From what curled starting position can you easily change to your different shape? (For example, crouched on both feet; lying on side; lying on back; kneeling; tightly curled on both shoulders.)

3 A sequence of three parts, curled and not curled, neatly and slowly joined together, would be very interesting.

Arms

1 Can you show me two or three ways to take all the weight on to your hands? (For example, 'kicking horses'; bunny jumps; cartwheels (illustrated); handstands.)

2 Remember to keep both arms straight for a safe, strong position.

3 Keep your hands and your head looking forwards.

Apparatus Work
16 minutes

1 Travel all around the room, changing smoothly from one way of moving to a new one. Do not touch any apparatus yet, but you may go over, across, under, along or in and out.

2 Start in a still, nicely balanced position on the floor. Travel up to and on to a piece of apparatus, and show me a neat, still, balanced position. Then move away from the apparatus to a new starting position on the floor, and begin again at the next piece of apparatus.

3 Travel on apparatus and floor, showing your shapes clearly. (For example, curled up rolls; stretched pulls on plank and bench; tucked up bunny jumps over bench or low barbox; star or stretched jumps up and from all apparatus.)

4 Can you travel all over the room, showing me your favourite ways to travel up to, on to, along and from apparatus?

5 On the apparatus, I would like to see travelling across, around, under, along, up and down – lots of variety, using the many different body actions you have practised, learned and enjoyed, I hope, this year.

Final Floor Activity
2 minutes

Stand tall and still. Lower slowly to sitting. Rock backwards with head on chest and back nicely rounded. Clasp hands under knees. Roll to one side, right over on to your front, jump up and repeat.

Gymnastic Activities

Teaching notes and NC guidance
Development over 4 lessons

Floorwork

Legs

1 Like sentries, pupils can go forwards and backwards in their own space corridor of 3–4 metres, not being disturbed by or disturbing others.

2 Shape is often dictated by what the arms are doing – at sides, stretched up, out to sides or forwards. The jump shape will be a long stretch, wide star, curled tuck, or (difficult) jack-knife.

3 The 'take off and landing' refer to the jump. This could be from one or both feet, landing with both feet together or apart, one foot in front of the other, or one foot landing after the other.

Body

1 'Everyone curl up tight and small. Keep your chin on your chest. Elbows in, round back.' Give this starting challenge, letting pupils choose their own bases to be curled on. If the response is poor, they can copy one of the class or the teacher.

2 The varied starting positions can be identified and looked at as ideas for the changes.

3 Particularly attractive is a sequence where the stretching is to different levels. (For example, curled crouch on both feet to high stretched standing; back to same curl; lower to low stretch, lying on back; curl on side; up to kneeling, stretching arms to a medium level in space.)

Arms

1 'All weight on hands' means that feet have to leave the floor at some point. During the past year, on floor and on apparatus, pupils will have done this often and seen good examples.

2 'Correct' technique needs to be continually checked. Arms that bend are weak and will give way. A straight arm is a safe prop.

3 If you look back under your arms, everything appears to be upside down. 'Head looking forwards' is even more important when taking weight on hands only, on apparatus.

Apparatus Work

1 At this stage of the year, pupils should be able to show neat, well-controlled, well-spaced, varied travelling on floor. Negotiating of apparatus, without touching it, is also required here.

2 Balanced start; travel; balanced finish, going from apparatus to apparatus, challenges pupils to make quick decisions to cope with different situations.

3 Be aware of making a shape at all times. If we make it a firm, whole-body shape (not lazy or sagging) the work becomes more demanding and the performance is greatly enhanced.

4 All gymnasts have their favourite routines that they enjoy doing almost without thinking. The teacher has to look out for, praise and coach the actions being presented, so that the 'favourite' is also the best routine.

5 Reception pupils often start school with little experience of the climbing, swinging, circling, jumping, hanging under, pulling and sliding that are typical in a lively Gymnastic Activities lesson. It is hoped that they are now less inhibited, more confident and more skilful at all these natural body movements.

Final Floor Activity

The sideways roll is a half turn from being on the back to being on the front. The impetus for the sideways roll comes from a swing of both bent knees to one side.

Dance

The Aims of Dance

Education has been described as the 'structuring of experiences in such a way as to bring about an increase in human capacity'. Dance aims to increase human capacity under the following headings:

1 **Physical development**. We focus on body action to develop skilful, well-controlled, versatile movement. We want our pupils to move well, looking poised and confident. The vigorous actions in dance also promote healthy physical development, fitness and strength.

2 **Knowledge and understanding**. Pupils learn and understand through the combination of physical activity (with its doing, feeling and experiencing of movement) and the mental processes of decision-making, as they plan, refine, evaluate and then plan again for improvement.

3 **Enjoyment**. Dance is fun and an interesting, sociable, enjoyable physical activity. In addition to the perspiration and deep breathing which the vigorous physical activity inspires, there should be smiling faces expressing enjoyment. When asked why they like something, pupils' first answer is usually 'It's fun!' It is hoped that enjoyable, sociable and physical activity experienced regularly at school in dance and other physical education lessons, can have an influence on pupils' eventual choice of lifestyle, long after they have left school. We want them to understand that regular physical activity makes you look and feel better, and helps to make you feel relaxed, calm and fit.

4 **Confidence and self-esteem**. Particularly at primary school, a good physical education that recognises and praises achievement can enhance an individual's regard for him or herself, and help to improve confidence and self-esteem. Dance lessons are extremely visual and offer many opportunities to see improvement, success and creativity; demonstrating these admirable achievements to others; and helping pupils feel good about themselves.

5 **Social development**. Friendly, co-operative social relationships are part of most dance lessons. Achievement, particularly in the 'dance climax' part of the lesson, is usually shared with a partner or a small group. Pupils also share space sensibly with others; take turns at working; demonstrate to, and watch demonstrations by, others; and make appreciative, helpful comments to demonstrators and partners.

6 **Creativity**. It has been said that 'if you have never created something, you have never experienced satisfaction.' Dance is a most satisfying activity, regularly challenging pupils to plan and present something original. Opportunities abound for an appreciative teacher to say 'Thank you for your demonstration and your own, original way of doing the movements.'

7 **Expression and Communication**. In dance we communicate through the expression in movement of the feelings or the action. We use, for example, stamping feet to express anger; we skip, punch the air or clap hands to show happiness; we swagger, head held high, to express self-assurance. Similarly, we create simple characters and stories by expressing them through movements associated with them. The old or young; machine or leaves; puppet, animal or circus clown, can all be expressed through their particular way of moving.

8 **Artistic and aesthetic appreciation**. Gaining knowledge and understanding of the quality-enhancing elements of movement is a particular aim of dance. Such understanding of quality, variety and contrast in the use of body action, shape, direction, size, speed and force, is a major contributor to appreciation of good movement. We want our pupils to understand what is good about good movement.

Stimuli as Starting Points with which to Inspire Dance Action

Stimuli are used to gain the interest of the class, provide a focus for their attention, get them into the action quickly, and inspire in them a desire for movement.

A dance stimulus is something you:

○ **enjoy doing**, such as natural actions. Pupils will immediately start to walk, run, jump, skip, hop, bounce or gallop, whether accompanied by music, percussion, following the teacher/leader, or responding to an enthusiastic teacher calling out the actions.

○ **can hear**. Sounds that stimulate movement include:

   a   medium to quick tempo music, including folk dance music

   b   percussion instruments – tambourine, drum, cymbal, clappers

   c   body contact sounds – clapping hands, stamping feet, slapping body, clicking fingers

   d   rhythmically chanted phrases, words, place names or actions which can be shortened or elongated to inspire and accompany actions

   e   vocal sounds to accompany actions, on the spot and travelling as in 'toom, toom, toom' marching; 'boomp, boomp, boomp' bouncing; and 'tick, tock, tick, tock' slow stepping

   f   action songs, chanted rhymes and nursery rhymes.

○ **can see or imagine**. Objects like a leaf, branch, balloon, ball, bubble, puppet, rag doll, firework, can all be used to suggest movement ideas to children. Use of imagery and imagination helps to communicate what we are trying to express more clearly. 'Can you creep softly and slowly, as if you did not want to be heard, coming home late?'

○ **have seen on a visit, on television, or in a photograph**. Of particular interest to pupils are:

   a   zoo animals – penguins. elephants, dolphins, monkeys

   b   circus performers – jugglers, clowns, trapeze artists, acrobats, tightrope walkers

   c   seaside play – swimming, paddling, making sandcastles, plus movements of the waves

   d   children's playground activities – climbing, swinging, sea-saw, throwing and catching, skipping, circling on a roundabout.

○ **experience seasonally** – spring and growth, summer holidays, autumn and harvest, winter snow and frost, Guy Fawkes' Night, Halloween, Christmas toys, circus and pantomime, Easter eggs.

○ **consider newsworthy or of human interest** – Olympic Games, extremes of weather, newly arrived pupils, hobbies, family, friendship, approaching holidays.

Whatever the starting point, the teacher must convert it into the language of movement. Children cannot 'be' leaves, but they can 'Travel on tip toes with light, floating movements, tilting and turning slowly.' They cannot 'be' clowns, but they can 'Do a funny walk on heels, spin round with one leg high, fall down slowly, bounce up and repeat.' They cannot 'be' machines, but they can 'Try pushing down actions, like corks into bottles, on the spot, turning or moving along, as on an assembly line.'

The Creative Dance Lesson Plan

Warming-up Activities which start the lesson are important because they can create an attentive, co-operative, industrious and thoughtful start to the lesson, put the class in the mood for dance, and encourage them to move with good body poise and tension, sharing the floor unselfishly. The activities need to be simple enough to get the whole class working, almost immediately, often by following the teacher who, ideally, is a stimulating **'purveyor of action'** enthusiastically leading the whole class, often by example, into wholehearted participation in simple activities which need little explanation. Some form of travelling, using the feet, is often the warming-up activity, with a specific way of moving being asked for. It might be to show better use of space, greater variety, greater control, good poise and body tension, or simply an enthusiastic use of all the body parts to warm up.

The Movement Skills Training middle part of the lesson is used to teach and develop the movement skills and patterns that are to be used in the new dance. Here, the teacher is an **educator**, informing, challenging, questioning, using demonstrations and sometimes direct teaching.

a Kneel down and curl to your smallest shape. Show me how you can start to grow, very slowly. Are you starting with your back, head, shoulders, elbows or arms? Show me clearly how you rise to a full, wide stretch position.

b If gesturing is like speaking with your body's movement, how might your body gesture say 'I am angry'? Stamp feet, clench fists, punch the air, jump up and down heavily.

c How are bubbles (made by teacher and pupils) moving? Where are they going? Floating gently, gliding smoothly, soaring from low to higher, sinking slowly.

The creating and performing Dance Climax of the lesson is the most important part and must not be missed out or rushed. If necessary, earlier parts of the lesson should be reduced. Here the teacher is a **coach**, helping and guiding the pupils as they work at their creation, moving round to all parts of the room to advise, encourage, enthuse, praise and, eventually, demonstrate.

a Slowly, start to grow and show me which parts are leading as you rise to your full, wide flower shape in our 'Spring Dance'. You might even twist your flower shape to look at the sun.

b Find a partner for our 'Gestures' dance and decide who is asking a favour by gesturing with body actions to say 'Please! I'm desperate! I need it! I must have it!' The other partner's body actions are saying 'Never! You must be joking! Go away!' When we look at demonstrations later, we will decide who the most expressive winners are.

c For our 'Bubbles dance', I will say the four actions that are to be practised – floating gently, gliding smoothly, soaring, sinking slowly, and you will show me how you have planned to dance them.

Depending on its complexity, a dance lesson will be repeated three or four times to allow sufficient time for repetition, practice and improvement to take place, and a satisfactory performance to be achieved and presented.

It has been said that 'dance is all about making, remembering and repeating patterns.'

Whether we are performing a created dance or an existing folk dance, there will still be a still start and finish, and an arrangement of repeated parts within.

The Traditional Folk Dance Lesson Plan – 30 minutes

Warming-up Activities (5 minutes). These varied steps can relate to the new figures to be taught, or they can be travelling steps or steps on the spot of any kind, to stimulate quick, easy enjoyable action to put the class in the mood for dance. The warm-up can be done alone or with a partner. As well as inspiring action, the teacher establishes high standards of neat footwork and good, safe, unselfish sharing of space. For example, 'Skip by yourself, to visit all parts of the room, keeping in time with the music.' 'When drum sounds twice, join hands with the nearest person and dance together.' 'When drum sounds once, dance by yourself again.'

Teach Figures of New Dance (14 minutes). Teaching is easier in a big circle formation where everyone can see and copy the teacher. Often, all can perform the whole dance together, slowly and carefully, figure by figure, practising it to the teacher's voice, then doing it at the correct speed. The teacher's non-stop vocal accompaniment, along with the actions, serves to remind the class of the actions and keeps them moving at the correct speed. For example, 'Everyone ready... Skip to the centre, 2, 3, turn on 4; back to places, 2, 3, arrive on 4. Boys to centre, 2, 3, turn on 4; back to places, 2, 3, there on 4. Girls to centre, 2, 3, turn on 4; back to places, 2, 3, hands joined on 4. All circle left, 2, 3, 4, 5, 6, back the other way; circle right, 2, 3, 4, 5, 6, ready to start again.'

Teaching in sets of two, three, four or more couples is more difficult because the sets are separate, with someone's back to the teacher. Each leading couple in turn will be taken slowly through the figures, then walking, then dancing to the music or the teacher's vocal accompaniment.

Teach The New Dance (7 minutes). Ideally, the new dance will be performed without stopping, helped by early reminders to the next dancers from the teacher's continuous vocal accompaniment. It is sometimes necessary to stop the music after each dancing couple has completed the dance, because of problems experienced by some of the dancers. The new couples are put in position, the music is re-started, and they do the dance once again.

Revise A Favourite Dance (4 minutes). This last dance, often chosen by pupils, should be a contrast to the lesson's new dance, for variety. A lively circle dance, with all dancing non-stop, can be contrasted with a set dance where only one or two of the four couples are dancing at a time.

Teaching Dance with 'Pace'

High on the list of accolades for an excellent dance lesson is the comment that 'It had excellent pace' and moved along, almost non-stop, from start to finish. Lesson pace is determined by the way that each of the several skills making up the whole lesson is taught. For example:

1   **Quickly into action**. Using few words, explain the skill clearly and challenge the class to begin. 'Show me your best stepping, in time with the music. Begin!' This near-instant start is helped if the teacher joins in and works enthusiastically with them.

2   **Emphasise the main teaching points, one at a time, while class is working**. The class all need to be working quietly if the teacher is to be heard. 'Visit all parts of the room – sides, ends and corners, as well as the middle.' 'Travel along straight lines, never following anyone.' (Primary school pupils always travel in a big anti-clockwise circle, all following one another, unless taught otherwise.)

3   **Identify and praise good work while the class is working**. The class teacher does not say 'well done' without being specific and explaining what is praiseworthy. Comments are heard by all and remind the class of key points. 'Well done, Emily. Your tip toe stepping is lively and neat.' 'Daniel, you keep finding good spaces to travel through. Well done.'

4   **Teach for individual improvement, while the class is working**. 'Michael, swing arms and legs with more determination, please.' 'Rachel, use your eyes each time you change direction to see where the best space is.'

5   **Use a demonstration, briefly**, to show good quality, or a good example of what is expected and worth copying. 'Stop, please, and watch Sophie, Michael, James and Kate step out firmly with neat, quiet footwork, never following anyone.' 'Stop and watch how Ellie is mixing bent, straight and swinging leg actions for variety.'

6   **Very occasionally, to avoid using too much activity time, a short demonstration is followed by comments from observers**. 'Half of the class will watch the other half. Look out for and tell me whose stepping is neat, lively and always well spaced. Tell me if someone impresses you for any other reason.' The class watch for about 12 seconds and three or four comments are listened to. For example: 'John is mixing tiny steps with big ones.' 'Sophie is stepping with feet passing each other, then with feet wide apart.' Halves of the class change over and repeat the demonstrations with comments.

7   **Thanks are given to all the performers and to those who made helpful, friendly comments**. Further practice takes place with reminders of the good things seen and commented on.

National Curriculum requirements for Dance – Key Stage 1: The Main Features

'The government believes that two hours of physical activity a week, including the National Curriculum for Physical Education and extra-curricular activities, should be an aspiration for all schools. This applies to all key stages.'

Programme of study

Pupils should be taught to:

a   use movement imaginatively, responding to stimuli, including music, and performing basic skills (e.g. travelling, being still, making a shape, jumping, turning, gesturing)

b   change the rhythm, speed, level and direction of their movements

c   create and perform dances using simple movement patterns, including those from different times and cultures

d   express and communicate ideas and feelings.

Attainment targets

Pupils should be able to demonstrate that they can:

a   select and use skills, actions and ideas appropriately, applying them with co-ordination and control

b   copy, explore, repeat and remember skills, and link them in ways that suit the activities

c   talk about differences between their own and others' work; suggest improvements; and use this understanding to improve their performance.

Main NC headings when considering assessment, progression and expectation

Planning – mostly before performing, but planning also takes place during performance, with pupils making quick decisions to find a space or adapt a skill. In these initial, exploratory stages, pupils try things out and learn from early efforts. When planning is satisfactory, there is evidence of understanding of the task; good use of own ideas; and consideration for others sharing the space.

Performing and improving performance – always the main outcome to be achieved. When performing is satisfactory, there is evidence of well-controlled, neat, safe and thoughtful work; a capacity for almost non-stop work, alone and with others; and simple skills being performed accurately and linked together with increasing control.

Linking actions – pupils build longer, 'joined-up' sequences of linked actions in response to the task set and stimuli used. In the same way that joined-up words make language and joined-up notes make music, joined-up actions produce movement sequences, ideally with a clear and obvious beginning, middle and end.

Reflecting and making judgements – pupils describe what they and others have done; talk about what they liked in a performance; and then make practical use of this reflection to improve. Where standards in evaluating are satisfactory, there is evidence of accurate observation and awareness of the actions; understanding of differences and similarities seen in demonstrations; awareness of key features and ways to achieve and improve them; and sensitive concern for others' feelings when discussing them.

Reception Dance Programme

Pupils should be able to:

Autumn	Spring	Summer
1 Listen to the teacher, then respond quietly and quickly.	**1** Work hard, almost without stopping, to improve and remember skills.	**1** Work with increasing skill and confidence, expressed in neat, quiet, poised performances.
2 Improve basic travelling actions – walk, run, jump, hop, skip, bounce, slide, gallop.	**2** Respond to rhythmic accompaniment, keeping in time with the music.	**2** Be keen to practise, almost non-stop, until asked to stop and change to a new activity.
3 Use whole-body movements thoughtfully to experience the varied actions possible.	**3** Develop poise, control and good balance in travelling, jumping, landing, stillness and whole-body stretching and bending.	**3** Be aware of the importance of good poise and clear body shapes in enhancing a performance.
4 Use whole-body movements whole-heartedly, using joints and muscles to their limit.	**4** Respond rhythmically to set tasks, with short, repeating patterns and sequences of movement.	**4** Be aware of the importance of good use of own space and whole room in adding variety and contrast to the work, and making space for others sharing the hall with you.
5 Use movements in isolated parts of the body, focusing on ways in which each can perform – feet, hands, arms, legs, back, head and shoulders.	**5** Use body parts in a variety of ways to add contrast and interest – different shape, direction, speed and effort.	**5** Practise simple, traditional dance steps and figures and use them in simple circle dances where all can see and copy the teacher.
6 Respond to varied stimuli – teacher, drum, music, poem, song, imagery: 'bubbles', 'ball', 'puppet', 'robot'.	**6** Learn simple, traditional dance steps and figures and use them in simple, circle, folk-style dances.	**6** Learn to link a series of actions together, rhythmically, in a short, repeating pattern.
7 Watch with interest to learn from others.	**7** Skip alone and with a partner to folk dance music, feeling and keeping to the 8-count phrasing typical of this music.	**7** Respond to varied stimuli – folk dance music, poem, song, imagery, nature, approaching holidays.
8 Be body-shape aware, still and moving, using whole body in firm, poised posture.	**8** Use imagery widely as a stimulus to actions – 'like a bubble, gently floating; slowly turning, sinking'.	**8** Express feelings and ideas through body movement – the wonder of natural birth and growth in spring.
9 Share space well so that all can practise freely, understanding 'own space' and 'whole room space'.	**9** Respond to varied stimuli – drum, music, poem, song, nursery rhyme, imagery, body-contact sounds.	**9** Link actions together neatly with a still start and finish, and a neat, well-planned middle.
10 Co-operate with a partner, leading, following, copying, combining and commenting on their work.	**10** Enjoy linking a series of simple actions and building them into an easily remembered, repeating pattern.	**10** Co-operate with a partner, leading, following, observing, coaching.
11 Celebrate Christmas with a seasonal dance.	**11** Watch a demonstration and be able to say what was pleasing and possibly worth copying.	**11** Create a seasonal 'Holidays' dance.
		12 Be an interested and encouraging observer, with helpful comments.

Year R

Lesson Plan 1 • 25 minutes
September

Theme: *Training class to listen, respond, concentrate and work together. The emphasis is on whole-body movements and movements possible in isolated parts of the body. This total concentration on the teacher within whole-class teaching is in contrast with most of their informal experiences at the start of the infant school.*

Warm-up and Body-training Activities
18 minutes

1 Begin by standing in a circle, hands joined, and able to see the teacher who sings and leads the class through the big actions:
   Let's join hands in one big ring,
   Let's join hands and let us sing,
   Let's join hands, both high and low, (reaching up, then down)
   Let's drop hands and wave 'Hello!' (repeat, with all singing)

2 What lovely singing and arm movements. Well done. Now put your hands together and stretch them right up to the ceiling – as big as a house.

3 Now, small as a mouse, bend down to touch the floor with your hands.

4 Move with me and say the words please. Big as a house and small as a mouse (illustrated). Big as a house – big stretch up on tiptoes. Small as a mouse – knees bent, hands on the floor. Once again, say the words and do the actions for me, please.

5 Let's use our hands again. Clap and count with me. Clap, 2, 3, 4, 5, 6, 7, 8; 1, 2, 3, 4, 5, 6, 7, stop!

6 Let's all use our feet now, and go for a little walk, keeping in time with my drum beat. You can follow me if you like. 1, 2, 3, 4, 5, 6, 7, 8; walk, 2, 3, 4, 5, 6, 7, 8; march, 2, 3, 4, 5, 6, 7, stop!

7 That was very good and most of you stopped when the drum told you to. Some of you followed the drum and me, and some of you went walking by yourselves.

Dance – Clapping and Stepping
7 minutes

1 Let's make a little 'Clapping and Stepping' dance, and see if you can be brilliant, standing, clapping with me when the drum isn't beating, for eight counts, then marching about when the drum is sounding for another eight counts.

2 Ready... begin! Stand and clap, stand and clap, 5, 6, 7, 8; march, march, with the drum, 5, 6, 7, 8; stand and clap, stand and clap, 5, 6, 7, 8; drum and steps, drum and steps, 5, 6, 7, 8.

3 Stop! That was excellent. Let's have a last practice and this time we'll make our clapping hands reach higher and higher, and we'll swing our arms smartly as we walk about. Ready... begin!

4 Finally, half the class watch the other half to experience the pleasure of performing and being praised and thanked, often with applause from observers.

Dance

Teaching notes and NC guidance
Development over 2 lessons

Aids to ensuring that pupils behave, listen and respond will include:

a starting in a circle formation where all can see and be seen by the teacher

b total concentration on the teacher and what is being said and done by the teacher. This concentration is essential after the informality and freedom while changing and getting ready for the lesson, and, possibly, during the previous lesson

c specific, clearly understood instructions and images, and their repetition, which the pupils enjoy

d the security and understanding provided by clear accompaniment by the teacher

e the friendly 'togetherness' of a lesson with plenty of variety – action song, big body movements and praise for equally enthusiastic participation and effort.

Warm-up and Body-training Activities

1 This is a near-instant start – make the circle; join the hands; sing and move to the words. It helps if the teacher sings one line at a time, slowly, while pupils listen, then repeats the line with the class joining in.

2 The participating teacher-leader, still with them in the circle, is now inspiring the good-quality, whole-hearted, whole-body actions that we are always aiming to produce in our Physical Education lessons.

3 Imagery – small as a mouse, big as a house – encourages the really small and really big contrasting actions of this dance. Such use of the imagination helps to communicate more clearly what we are trying to express.

4 This repetition of the words and the accompanying actions includes further teaching points such as 'big stretch up on tiptoes'.

5 From the joining, reaching up and down, and waving of hands in the starting song, we now use our hands for clapping in eight-count phrases.

6 Feet travelling, also in eight-count phrases, to the drum accompaniment, and responding well to a rhythmic accompaniment, keeping in time with it, is a pleasing progression.

7 Praise for a successful practice, often accompanied by a short demonstration by a small group, delights those who are asked to demonstrate, and gives others ideas to use and copy.

Clapping and Stepping Dance

The created dance climax of the lesson is the most important part and must always be given its full allocation of the lesson time, even if this means reducing earlier parts of the lesson.

1 The preliminary explanation and reminder of the two parts of the dance are most important. When the drum is silent, the class make clapping sounds. When the drum sounds, class hands are silent, but feet are travelling. In both we use an eight-count rhythm.

2 'Rhythmicising', singing out the actions by the teacher, is widely used in dance teaching, both to remind the class of the actions, and to keep them together at the correct speed.

3 Prior to the next practice, coaching of the main points, involving body parts and space awareness, adds interest and quality to the performance.

4 Performance, observed by half of class and teacher, inspires the very best work.

Lesson Plan 2 • 25 minutes
September

Theme: *Focusing attention on the teacher, their bodies and the start/stop of the drum as they perform their movements together.*

Warm-up and Body-training Activities
18 minutes

1   Begin with everyone sitting in a circle, spaced apart, and able to see and copy the teacher's actions and singing. Legs are straight out in front. Big arm movements as pupils touch named parts to accompany each line:
Heads and shoulders, knees and toes,
knees and toes, knees and toes,
Heads and shoulders, knees and toes,
we all clap hands together.

2   Well done. Lots of good actions and singing. Let's do it again with really high touches on top of the head and shoulders, and a big bend forwards to touch the knees and toes. Ready... Heads and shoulders, knees and toes, knees and toes, knees and toes. Heads and shoulders, knees and toes, we all clap hands together.

3   Stand up now, please. Watch how I do tiny bounces with my feet just leaving the floor. Can you try it, letting your toes just leave the floor? Do it with me, like a ball bouncing low (illustrated). Bounce, bounce, tiny bounce, 5, 6, once again; 1, 2, 3, 4, bouncing low, bouncing low; 1, 2, 3, 4, 5, 6, 7, stop!

4   Listen to the drum and do tiny running steps like a rolling ball, keeping in time with the drum. When the drum stops, be still and show me a small, rounded shape like a ball that uses your back and your arms. Ready... go! Run, run, run, 5, 6, 7 and still!

5   What rounded shape have you made? Are you using your back and your arms to look like a little ball? Once again, with the drum, 1, 2, 3, 4, run, run, run and stop! Round and still, like a little ball, please.

6   Let's practise again. Show me your still, round, starting shape where you listen for the starting signal, the drum sounding. Run carefully, looking for good spaces, until the drum does a loud beat to stop you. Be still and show me your best, little, rounded ball shape.

Dance — The Little Ball
7 minutes

1   We can call our dance 'The Little Ball'. Please stand, ready, in your own space. We will do eight little bounces like a ball. Then the drum sounds for us to run with tiny steps like a rolling ball. When the drum stops, be still and show me your best, round ball shape.

2   Ready... bounce, bounce, 3, 4, 5, 6, now the drum; run, run, run, run, 5, 6, make a small ball shape. Be still everybody so that I can see your round ball shape.

3   Well done, everyone. Let's have half of the class sitting and looking at the other half. Look out for and tell me about good bounces, good running and nice round shapes.

Dance

Teaching notes and NC guidance
Development over 2 lessons

The main aim for Physical Education is to make pupils become physically active, promoting normal, healthy growth and physical development. The appropriate physical activity for this young age group is inspired by teaching that includes:

a   starting in a circle formation where all can easily see and focus on the teacher

b   specific exercises to develop body awareness by isolating individual parts and concentrating on them: 'Heads and shoulders, knees and toes...'

c   specific exercises to produce whole-body movements, such as full stretches and bends, using joints and muscles to their limit for proper development

d   the use of song to focus attention, produce action and bring the class formally together at the start of the lesson. Song also develops language skills and vocabulary as pupils feel, at first hand, the meanings of words

e   repetition and clear accompaniment by the teacher

f   good use of imagery to communicate an idea: 'Little bounces, just like a ball bouncing low'; 'Be still and small in a round, ball shape.'

g   enthusiastic, encouraging teaching by a teacher who gives the impression – 'This is fun.'

Warm-up and Body-training Activities

1   Instant start, seated in a big circle, all able to see and copy the teacher. The song is so easy and repetitive that pupils can start, straight away, singing the words with the teacher and copying the actions. Singing very slowly helps their accompaniment and their performance.

2   Asking for bigger and better quality actions during repetitions of the action song is always part of what we mean by 'Lesson Development'.

3   Good use of imagery stimulates pupils' imagination, giving them an excellent mental picture of what is wanted. Using the balls of the feet, ankles and knees to make the bounces and the soft, squashy landings is best illustrated by using good performers.

4   The eight-count, repeating pattern of the bouncing, is now used during the tiny running steps to the sounding of the drum. As always, we do not want the class to travel in an anti-clockwise circle, all following one another, typical of most classes. 'Run on straight lines, never following anyone. If they stop suddenly, you might bump into them.'

5   Body parts awareness now extends to a feel for different body shapes. Body shape is an ever-present feature of movement and after initially considering 'What are the actions and the body parts involved?' we progress to asking 'What are the clear body shapes that best improve this performance?'

6   The teacher's 'rhythmicising' reminder of the two sets of actions has also reminded pupils of the correct speed for the performance. A progression can be to let them do the bouncing and running without any vocal reminder from the teacher.

The Little Ball Dance

1   After their many practices of the whole dance, all they need now is a reminder of the eight silent bounces, followed by the eight tiny travelling steps, plus the still, round, ball shape end.

2   The teacher's 'rhythmicising' accompaniment keeps the whole class together.

3   In the half-watch-half performance, pupils can be challenged to keep their own time.

Lesson Plan 3 • 25 minutes
October

Theme: *Body shape, which is an ever-present feature within our movement, whether we are still or in motion. Still shapes that feel firm are physically demanding and need good body tension. Moving shapes should involve the whole body, particularly the spine.*

Warm-up Activities
4 minutes

1 All stand in a circle, spaced apart, and able to see and copy the teacher's actions as she or he recites the poem slowly:
My hands upon my head I place, on my shoulders, on my face;
On my hips I place them – so, then bend down to touch my toe;
Now I raise them up so high, make my fingers fairly fly,
Now I clap them, one, two, three, then I fold them silently.

2 Well done, everyone. Let's do these actions again. Hands are very clever, aren't they, as they touch and fly and clap. Ready...

3 Our feet are also very clever. Show me the soft bounces we did last time, like a little ball (low, quiet, with a 'give' in the knees).

4 Now skip to visit all parts of the room. Swing your arms and legs up in front of you in your lively skipping.

Movement Skills Training
15 minutes

1 Sit down in your own space. Our bodies are all making a shape, different to everyone else's. I will say 'Hold... change.' 'Hold' means you sit very still in your shape; 'Change' means you show me a different shape. Ready? Hold... change. Make a new shape. Hold... change. Hold, feel your muscles... change and hold.

2 This time you can sit or lie or stand or kneel to show me your interesting shapes. Ready... hold... and change. Hold, very still... and change. Try a stretched shape with your muscles working hard.

3 Now try a bent shape. Use your arms, your back and your legs. Can anyone do a twisted shape or a nice, round ball shape?

4 Keep doing your 'Hold!' and 'Change!' on your own, without me saying it. I would like to see you try a funny shape or a robot shape or even an upside-down shape. Keep working.

5 Thank you for all those brilliant, still shapes. Can you be clever now and make whole-body, travelling shapes as you tiptoe or walk in and out of one another, without touching anyone?

6 You can twist to circle around someone; stretch arms in front to go through a little space; stretch arms sideways like an aeroplane to turn a corner; or curl, small, travelling slowly, like a little ball.

Dance – Still and Moving Shapes
6 minutes

1 Let's do a small, still shapes dance and a moving shapes dance. Show me your best, still, starting shape. Feel your muscles.

2 Now travel with the tambourine beating, making your moving shapes, stretching, bending, wide or twisting, in and out of others and into spaces.

3 The loud bang means 'Hold!' your still shape until the tambourine starts asking you to travel again.

4 Continue to practise, and then half of the class watch the other half.

Dance

Teaching notes and NC guidance
Development over 2 lessons

Pupils should be taught the best possible posture and use of the body, using movements imaginatively as they travel, hold stillness and make shapes, for example. Development of body shape awareness and understanding is helped by:

a   starting in circle formation where all can see and easily follow the teacher's actions with total concentration

b   starting with a poem to provide a focus for pupils' attention and actions

c   isolating and concentrating on individual body parts to feel the many, varied ways that they can move

d   giving clear, specific instructions. 'Hold' means you sit still in your shape. 'Change' means you show a different shape

e   good use of imagery to clarify what is wanted – 'a ball shape; a robot shape; like an aeroplane; an upside-down shape.'

f   watching and learning from demonstrations by others, particularly when the demonstrations are accompanied by comments from the teacher

g   enthusiastic, encouraging teaching by a teacher who always stands, sits and moves with good posture.

Movement Skills Training

1   'Hold' and 'Change' is a good fun activity, guaranteed to hold pupils' attention as they think ahead to what their next shape will be, still sitting.

2   The next 'Hold' and 'Change' challenge is even better fun, as pupils move to new parts of their body on which to show their unusual, own created balances.

3   Examples of interesting bent, twisted and round shapes need to be demonstrated to give everyone good ideas and to encourage the creators.

4   Funny, or upside-down, or robotic shapes, held and changed, freely, but still on the spot, need almost non-stop, enthusiastic commentary from the teacher, describing what is seen.

5   Well-practised on the spot, the travelling shapes should be varied, as should the travelling.

6   As always, good use of imagery to stir pupils' imagination should produce many varied and original travelling body shapes, which will be worth looking at.

Still and Moving Shapes Dance

1   A repeating sequence of three or four still shapes, while on the spot, is recommended to provide contrast, variety and hard physical work holding strong, clear shapes. We want pupils to be able to remember, repeat and improve their sequences, and understand the meaning of, and elements within, 'Improvement'.

2   Travelling to the beat of the tambourine, with moving shapes, weaving in and out of others, needs lots of encouraging, accompanying comments from the teacher, making pupils aware of the brilliant ideas seen, so that others can learn from and even copy them.

3   The held still shape, signalled by the tambourine bang, keeps the travelling down to a few seconds, with the emphasis on the shapes used, before pupils set off again.

4   Knowing that there is a good chance that half will watch half as the lesson's climax makes most pupils prepare and practise as well as possible for the performance.

Lesson Plan 4 • 25 minutes
October

Theme: *Space awareness and understanding that we can move in our own personal space and the whole room. We share the space so that we can all enjoy moving, unrestricted by others.*

Warm-up Activities
4 minutes

1   Find a nice big space where you can move your arms without touching anyone. Pretend this space is a big bubble, which you can push to make bigger.

2   Reach up high, on tiptoes, with both hands and – push! Now, reach in front, to the sides, and even behind you – and push!

3   Who's good at balancing? Can you push to one side with your hands and push to the other side with a foot, at the same time?

4   With the music, let me see you leaving your bubble and skipping and dancing to all parts of the room (illustrated). When the music stops, get back inside your bubble. (Repeat several times.)

Movement Skills Training
15 minutes

1   Stand in your own big bubble. Show me how you can use different shapes to reach and push your bubble away. You can be long like a pencil, wide like a star, or you can twist to reach behind you.

2   Keep working, please, doing three or four different shapes, reaching to many parts of your own space. You can reach with hands and feet, sometimes using both at the same time.

3   Well done. I saw lots of big, strong shapes pushing bubbles out to make your own space grow. Now the music will help you to travel into the big space of the whole room. Off you go.

4   Stop. When the music starts this time, can you remember to visit all parts of the room – the sides, ends and the middle, never following anyone? Off you go.

5   Stop. Most of us are only using our feet as we travel, walking, running or skipping. Can you try some big, travelling shapes this time, like we did in our last lesson? Think about what your whole body looks like. I will be looking for stretched, wide, curled and twisted shapes. Go.

Dance — Bubbles
6 minutes

1   Find a partner who will stand next to you, in your shared bubble. Decide which one of you will be number one, and which number two. Hands up, number one... Hands up, number two... Good.

2   Number one, stay in the bubble, reaching to all the spaces above, to the sides and behind you, to make your space bigger. Number two, travel with the music, visiting lots of room spaces and going around all the other bubbles. I will ask you to return to your partner and your own bubble again. When the music stops, you and your partner will hold your best, still shape.

3   Well done, partners. Now we change over. Number two stays in the bubble, and number one goes travelling to the music. Remember – whole body shapes in your own personal space and in the big room space.

4   Let's try the whole dance twice through with a short stop after the first time. Show a good starting shape. Begin.

5   Half the class watch the other half to see good spacing, actions and firm shapes.

Dance

Teaching notes and NC guidance
Development over 2 lessons

Pupils should be taught to be mindful of others and share space sensibly. Being 'mindful of others' is best developed by including:

a an awareness of one's own personal space, including the parts we seldom reach – behind, out to the sides and high overhead, in addition to the well-frequented space in front

b the recognition that sufficient 'own space' is essential for satisfactory, safe activity

c good use of imagery to clarify the extent of one's own surrounding space: 'Pretend the space is a big bubble.'

d an awareness of the whole room, shared space, and the desirable way to travel within it to ensure minimum interruption to others' movement. Pupils of all primary school ages will travel anti-clockwise in a big circle, impeding and being impeded by those immediately behind and in front of them unless taught to travel otherwise: 'Visit all parts of the room – the sides, ends and the middle, never following anyone.'

e praise for those trying hard to 'share the space sensibly and unselfishly.'

f activity with a partner to experience the fun and the pleasure of working with someone, planning interesting new activities that you cannot do on your own.

Warm-up Activities

1 Finding a big space 'where you can move your arms without touching anyone' is always a good way to start any Physical Education lesson.

2 Reaching into spaces seldom, if ever, reached into is also an excellent exercise for developing whole body mobility.

3 Travelling inside your bubble makes you conscious of the need to look for a real space by using your eyes before using your feet.

4 Pupils can be asked to pretend that they are leaving footprints everywhere in the room, not only in the usual, anti-clockwise circle, nowhere near the sides, ends or even the middle.

5 Whole-body travelling shapes need all the air spaces, above, in front, behind, and wide to the sides, to be pierced by the arms.

Bubbles Dance

1 In a dance lesson about 'Space Awareness', check that all couples about to start the dance are well spaced apart from all others. Couples starting in an excellent space can be praised because that will be their good team space for the dance.

2 Number one stays in his or her starting space to work at making this space even larger. Number two, the traveller, goes in and out of all the other bubbles, stationary and moving. Travellers return to team starting places when asked to by the teacher. The music is stopped when pairs are re-united, side by side, holding a clear, firm, body shape.

3 Before the change-over of duties, good ideas seen by the teacher, stationary and travelling, can be shared in a short demonstration.

4 A still start, holding a clear body shape; an interesting middle with clear shapes and varied use of directions and levels; and a still finish with firm shapes is followed by the second performance after partners change over duties.

5 Half watch half, looking for big, firm body shapes and reaching to many places in space.

Lesson Plan 5 • 25 minutes
November

Theme: *Travelling with neat footwork, varied actions and use of feet and legs as pupils walk, run, jump, skip, bounce, gallop and slide.*

Warm-up Activities
4 minutes

1   All stand in a big circle, ready to do some travelling actions. We will all sing the words and do the actions:
    This is the way we walk to school, walk to school, walk to school,
    This is the way we walk to school, on a cold and frosty morning.
    This is the way we skip in the hall, skip in the hall, skip in the hall,
    This is the way we skip in the hall, on a cold and frosty morning.

2   That was very good. Let's do it again. Pretend it is a cold and frosty morning and we need to do lively actions to keep warm.

Movement Skills Training
15 minutes

1   I am going to follow the drum as it tells me what kind of actions to do. Would you like to follow it with me?

2   It says, march like a soldier and swing your arms. Now tiptoe with quiet, tiny steps, and arms not moving very much. Now skip and skip and swing your arms. Feet together, bounce along, 1, 2, 3, 4. Slide your feet along the floor, reaching forwards as you go. And gallop and gallop, 3, 4, lift your feet high off the floor. Run, run, run and jump; run, run, run and jump.

3   Well done. That was good fun, following the drum leader. We need to practise again and try to space apart better. Pretend you each have a drum leader, looking for and taking you to good big spaces where you won't bump into anyone.

4   Show me a beautiful, ready-to-start shape. I will tell you the actions. Keep in time with the drum. Marching... Tiptoe steps... Skips... Bounces... Gallops... Run and jump, run and jump, and stop! Show me your still, finishing shape.

Dance — Follow The Drum
6 minutes

1   For our dance, let's do 'Follow the Drum'. The drum will beat at different speeds with stops in between the actions for you to show a strong, still shape, ready for the next action.

2   Listen for the drum, then start performing the action I tell you. When the drum stops, you stop. Show me a neat, still starting shape. Ready... now! (Short, 10–12 second beat, followed by the louder beat which says 'Stop!' The still, held shape period before the next and different drum beat should be about four seconds, long enough for an infant to hold the shape.)

3   That was excellent. All sit down, listen to the drum and tell me what actions you think it is playing. (Hopefully, they will give correct answers – 'Galloping! ... Walking! ... Skipping! ... Sliding! ... Bouncing!' and be told 'Yes, well done.')

4   Stand up and show me your still, starting shape. This time I will not be telling you the different actions. Start and stop with the drum. Make your actions fit the sound each time.

Dance

Teaching notes and NC guidance
Development over 2 lessons

The prime aim of all Physical Education lessons is to inspire vigorous, whole body, physically challenging activity. In addition to promoting normal, healthy growth we want our pupils to have well-controlled, neat, poised and versatile movement. These aims are assisted by:

a   starting together in a circle, with a song focusing on some of the ways we can 'travel'

b   a lively teacher accompaniment, giving a picture of the right ways to walk, skip and run, with repetitions of the song to let pupils improve their performances

c   good fun, follow the drum leader, specific travelling actions which keep changing for variety and to hold pupils' attention

d   praise for, and demonstrations of, actions that are neat, quiet, well-controlled and well-spaced

e   the attention-holding dance climax as pupils listen for and respond to the varying nature of the drumming.

Warm-up Activities

1   There is an instant start, following the teacher-leader's lively, energetic actions and joining in the singing. The emphasis is on whole body, larger-than-life actions for winter.

2   Hands might be tucked under warm armpits for those actions where a lively arm swing is not so essential, as in walking. After they have all done it well, the teacher can ask, 'Can anyone suggest another lively action for keeping warm in winter?' and they might suggest, 'This is the way we chase outside,' or 'This is the way we bounce and twist.'

Movement Skills Training

1   Trying to follow the drum leader is an interesting and popular challenge.

2   The drum and teacher leaders vary the style of the actions to give the big strong march; the tiny, soft steps; the energetic skipping with high arm swings; the soft little bounces; the slow, long slides along the floor; the vigorous gallops, lifting high off the floor; and the longer favourite run, run, run and jump.

3   The teacher can be looking out, and praising, the dancer and pretend drum pairing whose use of floor space is as commendable as the quality of their travelling.

4   Prior to this next practice, the class can be coached: 'Strong arms swing as you march... high knees lifting in your skipping... good, strong ankle stretch in your bounces and soft, gentle, squashy landings... big high jump after your run, run, run.'

Follow the Drum Dance

1   For the first practice of their dance, there is a recurring still start, an action-filled middle, and a still finish. On each drum beat 'Stop!' pupils hold the body shape that they have just been using. The teacher makes them wait, listening attentively, for the start of the next short period of drum beat-inspired action.

2   The teacher is still reminding the class of the actions he or she is about to play for, and is continually asking for better quality, better controlled, poised actions.

3   Pupils listen to and try to identify the actions the drum is playing for.

4   Finally, they are challenged: 'You decide what actions the drum is playing for.'

Lesson Plan 6 • 25 minutes
November

Theme: *Body parts awareness, learning to understand and 'feel' the ways in which the whole body and its isolated parts can move.*

Warm-up Activities
4 minutes

1 Stand where you can all see me, in your own big space. Perform the actions of the song with me as I sing them slowly, and please help me with the singing:
   Two little hands go clap, clap, clap,
   Two little feet go tap, tap, tap,
   Two little hands go bump, bump, bump,
   Two little feet go jump, jump, jump,
   One little body turns around,
   One little child sits quietly down.

2 Well done. This time, can you show me how you can clap hands and bump hands high, or in front or to one side of you, as if you were reaching out in a big bubble?

Movement Skills Training
15 minutes

1 Stand by yourself with lots of space around you. Show me a huge stretch, up to the ceiling. Now collapse like a rag doll with arms and head hanging down. Now draw big circles in front of you, one way around, then back the other way.

2 Let's be clever and join these three whole-body movements together. Stretch up high to the ceiling; drop down like a rag doll; circle around with long arms; circle back the other way.

3 Excellent. One last practice and this time feel your whole body, arms, legs and back working as you move. Ready, begin.

4 Let's try moving only one body part, starting with your shoulders. Lift them both, then lower. Lift one, then lower. Lift the other, then lower. Pull them forwards, push them back. Circle them forwards, up and back.

5 Arms next. Stretch them, reaching in every direction. Bend them in and stretch them out again. Arms can make big circles. They can punch firmly... and shake loosely. Let them swing low from side to side.

6 Hands by themselves can clench and stretch; clap different parts of each other; come together slowly without a clap; explode apart quickly.

Dance — Follow My Leader
6 minutes

1 Find a partner and stand facing each other. Decide who is the leader and who will be the follower for our 'Follow My Leader' dance.

2 Leaders, you move, using one body part at a time, slowly, so that your partner can follow you easily (illustrated). Use those parts we have already practised – shoulders, arms and hands, and do only two or three actions with each, so that you can repeat and remember them.

3 Half of the partners will take turns to perform for the other half. Look out for and tell me about good actions you see in one body part only.

4 Thank you for your good, helpful demonstrations and comments. Next week, we will change over the leaders.

Dance

Teaching notes and NC guidance
Development over 2 lessons

Pupils should be able to show that they can improve performance, alone and with a partner. Such 'Improvement' is assisted by:

a the lesson having a start, middle and end with an obvious unity of purpose and with pupils understanding what that purpose is. This lesson is all about concentrating on isolated body parts and using them neatly and to the limits of their possible movement

b bringing the class together at the start with a song with actions to practise, repeat, improve and develop: 'Can you do your handclaps high, or in front, or to one side?' (Rather than only in front of you)

c specific coaching for quality, often with an accompanying demonstration, to clarify what is wanted: 'Show me a huge stretch, right up to the ceiling'

d the use of images to give a good picture of what is the ideal: 'Drop down like a rag doll'

e specific coaching by the teacher: 'Hands can clench, stretch, clap...'

f partner work, which necessitates thoughtful planning and decision-making when the leader, and provides new ideas when the follower

g learning from others' ideas during demonstrations.

Warm-up Activities

1 The teacher can demonstrate and speak each line, alone, then ask the class to join in.

2 If we aim for improvement through repetition, it is essential to ask for something better each time. From the good quality, body-parts actions start, we are now emphasising that improvement can be achieved through better and more varied use of the space we are in.

Movement Skills Training

1 'Lots of space around you' can be checked by moving long arms to sides and forwards, without impeding or being impeded by others.

2 This three-part sequence requires an awareness of the spine's high stretch, low collapse and medium level circlings.

3 Feet and legs will need to be apart, feeling strong, to provide a secure base.

4 A shoulder movement sequence of several parts will inspire many unusual actions.

5 Arm movements will lead to many varied, pleasing and novel sequences.

6 The many new hand movements being tried can be improved by a reminder: 'Try them at different levels, reaching into unusual parts of the space around you.'

Follow My Leader Dance

1 Emphasise that the leader is responsible for deciding the well-spaced start position as well as showing clear, firm, body-part movements throughout the dance.

2 Following partner watches and copies the few, repeating actions, leading eventually, ideally, to working in unison with the leader.

3 Same leaders lead this week, trying hard to have 'Our pair chosen for their good actions.'

Lesson Plan 7 • 30 minutes
December

Theme: *Christmas.*

CD TRACK 2

Warm-up Activities
4 minutes

1 Skip in your own space. Skip, skip, 3, 4, 5, 6, 7 and stop!

2 Clap hands in different spaces, high, low, in front or to one side. Clap, clap, 3, 4, clap, clap, 7 and 8. (Repeat skips and claps.)

3 Skip, travelling for six counts. On '7' and '8', face a partner to do gentle hand claps. Skip and travel, 3, 4, 5, 6, face a partner.

4 Clap hands with your partner for eight counts. Use one or both hands. Clap, clap, 3, 4, gently clap, skip again (...and clap).

5 Brilliant! For the last four claps, you may say 'Happy Christmas when it comes!' Go! Skip, skip, 3, 4, 5, 6, find a partner; clap, clap, 3, 4, Happy Christmas, when it comes! (Repeat.)

Movement Skills Training
14 minutes

1 March, swinging your arms proudly to the tambourine beat. When it shakes, do a marching turn on the spot and then move off again.

2 March, march, 3, 4, swing your arms, now we turn, turn, 3, 4, on the spot, then travel again. (Several repetitions for practice.)

3 Stand with body parts all loose and saggy, not like the firm body we had as we marched. Let head, shoulders and arms droop down in front of you. You feel as if you have no bones.

4 Now be slowly lifted by an invisible string tied to your hands. Reach hands right up above your head. Oh! Someone has cut the string and you collapse down again. (Repeat lift, drop.)

5 Lean forwards at the waist, arms out sideways like wings. Show me how you can fly, glide, hover and zoom to different spaces. Remember to tilt your body to one side when you turn.

6 Lean forwards from your waist with one arm hanging forwards and one arm hanging behind. Show me your slow, heavy, elephant way of walking, and your trunk and your tail.

Dance — Toy Factory
12 minutes

1 To start this seasonal story the teacher can close a door to represent the departure of the weary toy maker. The toys have a secret life, on their own, playing like children.

2 All practise the strong march, march and turn, turn of the soldier, with good arm swings.

3 Now, by contrast, the loose, hanging rag dolls are pulled up high by the imaginary string. They can rise straight up, slowly, with round back unrolling, or they can twist, alternate shoulder leading. Then they drop suddenly and surprisingly.

4 Aeroplanes need to be reminded to 'change speeds, directions and levels, always keeping your aeroplane shape. Fly to every part of the room.'

5 With heavy, slow steps, the elephants, feet wide apart for balance, lumber forwards, with interesting swings and swishes of trunk and tail.

6 Pupils can either decide which toy they want to be, or, to produce more equal-sized groups, be told which to be by the teacher.

7 Group after group, reminded by the teacher, fill the toy shop with all the varied actions.

8 Morning, and the sounds of the toy maker at the door, make them all go back to starting places, holding the many different, still, body shapes from the night before.

Dance

Teaching notes and NC guidance
Development over 3 lessons

Pupils should be able to show control in linking actions together in ways that suit the activities. We join notes to make music. We join words to make sentences. We join strokes of a brush, crayon or pencil to make art. We want our pupils to understand that they join actions to make 'movement'. The extent of the quality, variety and contrast within these 'joined-up' actions determines the extent of the achievement and progress. Developing control in linking actions is assisted by:

a   an easy to follow rhythm with enough repetitions of each of the two or three actions being joined: 'Skip and travel, 3, 4, 5, 6, 7, 8; clap, clap, 3, 4, clap, clap, 7, 8'

b   the teacher's vocal 'rhythm' accompanying the actions as a continual reminder of what is happening and what is about to happen: 'Skip and travel, 3, 4, 5 ,6, face a partner; clap hands gently, 3, 4, clap, clap, now skip again; skip, skip...'

c   an interesting variety in each of the sets of two actions being linked, again assisted by the teacher's rhythmic reminders: 'March, march, 3, 4, swing our arms, now we turn; turn, turn on the spot, 5, 6, march again'

d   the teacher understanding that a repeating pattern of two or three movements makes the pattern easy to remember, repeat and improve: 'Rag dolls hang all limp and loose; the strings now pull you tall and straight'; 'Elephants slowly walk along; then they swish their trunk and tail; elephants slowly walk along; then they slowly swish their trunk and tail.'

Warm-up Activities

1   An eight-count phrasing is often used in warm-up actions since it is long enough for several interesting things to happen.

2   The eight-count clapping sequence is long enough to let you reach to many places.

3, 4   Now we join the two sets of eight skips and claps, with a partner.

5   A seasonal greeting on the last four claps with partner can change with the seasons. 'Happy holiday in the sun!'

Movement Skills Training

1, 2   An instant start with teacher-leader drumming, marching, 3, 4; shaking, turning, 3, 4.

3, 4   Feet apart for good balance. Slowly lower, floppy head, neck, arms, spine, waist and legs, feeling all loose. Now reach up, unravelling from legs up through waist, spine, shoulders, arms to a high stretch being pulled by an imaginary string. Cut! Down again.

5   The favourite aeroplanes fill the hall with action, and in and out of one another flying.

6   The elephants' slow, lumbering movement is in contrast with the speedy, exciting planes.

Toy Factory Dance

1   One of the pupils can close the room door, signalling the toy maker's departure.

2–5   The class is asked to express the main character and personality of each of the toys through body movement. Each has a main feature through which to be recognised.

6, 7   Groups are reminded of the order, called in by the teacher, one at a time, then the whole toy shop is working at their larger than life actions, together as groups and as a class.

Lesson Plan 8 • 25 minutes
January

Theme: *Simple, traditional-style dance steps and figures.*

Warm-up Activities
5 minutes

1 Skip by yourself to visit every part of the room.

2 If your space is suddenly crowded, keep skipping on the spot, then travel on when there is plenty of room.

3 Skip for eight counts, join hands with a partner and dance for eight counts. Then separate and dance by yourself for eight counts. Then join with a different partner for the next eight counts. I will be counting to keep us all together.

4 By yourself, 3, 4, 5, 6, join a partner. Hands joined, 3, 4, 5, 6, 7, split up. By yourself, 3, 4, 5, 6, find a partner. Dance together, 3, 4, 5, 6, 7, split up. On your own, 3, 4, 5, 6, 7, 8.

Teach Steps and Figures of the Lesson's Folk Dance
14 minutes

1 Listen to this country-dance music. Let me hear you clapping your hands once to each bar of the music. I will count. You clap. Ready... 1... 2... 3... 4; clap... 2... 3... 4; clap... clap... clap... clap. Well done. Most of you are feeling the rhythm of the music.

2 Now let's see if you can skip in time with this lively music. Ready... skip and skip and skip and skip, 1 and 2 and 3 and 4 (several repetitions for practice).

3 Join hands in a big circle. Let's practise all walking forwards together for four counts, then carefully walking backwards, back to our starting places.

4 One more practice, with the music this time. Can you help me, please, by counting out for four forwards and four back, so that we all keep together? Ready... forwards, 2, 3, 4; back, 2, 3, again; in, 2, 3, 4; out, 2, 3 and stop. That was called 'into the centre and out again' in country dancing.

Dance – Traditional-style Circle Folk Dance
6 minutes

Music – any 32-bar English or Scottish country dance.

Formation – All stand in a circle with hands joined, and able to see and copy the teacher who is part of the circle.

Bars 1–8 All walk forwards into the centre for four counts, then all walk out backwards to your starting circle for four counts.

Bars 9–16 With hands by your sides, all skip forwards into the centre, then all skip back out to your starting places.

Bars 17–24 All bounce forwards into the circle, then bounce out again.

Bars 25–32 Join hands to make a big circle, all walk around, anti-clockwise, led by teacher. (Repeat.)

Dance

Teaching notes and NC guidance
Development over 2 lessons

'Pupils should be taught to perform movements or patterns, including some from existing dance traditions.' This welcome continuing requirement in the revised National Curriculum ensures a place for traditional as well as 'creative' dance for all primary school pupils. Both types of dance have their enthusiasts and supporters in a typical staff room. Both can now be mutually supportive, sharing ideas and dances.

For beginners in folk dance, the teacher concentrates on:

a   clapping to feel the timing of the music

b   teaching and practising the skipping travelling step by yourself and with a partner, using music that is quite brisk (the more expert the country dancer, the slower the music)

c   rhythmically accompanying the groups of eight steps to each eight-bar phrase of the music. This keeps pupils in time with the music and gives reminders – 'Skip by yourself, 3, 4, 5, 6, find a partner; skip together, 3, 4, 5, 6, now by yourself'

d   circle dances with simple actions; pupils copy the teacher, who joins in to demonstrate. At the simplest level, all the pupils perform throughout. These 'traditional-style' simple dances introduce the class to some of the steps and figures of the established dances.

Warm-up Activities

1   The teacher can set the rhythm for the skipping with his or her voice and/or by drumming.

2   Some might never have thought of dancing on the spot when it is suddenly crowded.

3   The teacher's 'rhythmicising' keeps the whole class together in their travelling and in their meetings. '1, 2, 3, 4, 5, 6, join a partner; dance together, 3, 4, 5, 6, on your own.'

4   Easy actions in a circle dance, led by the teacher, almost need no preliminary explanation. 'Walk in together, hands joined, 5, 6, 7, now back; walk back, hands joined, 5, 6, 7, again.'

Traditional-style Circle Folk Dance

Bars 1–8   In the 'hands joined' position in the circle, elbows are down with hands joined just above waist height for comfort. The teacher restrains any who would go charging in, pulling others off their feet. 'Let's keep this beautiful, round, circle shape, please.'

Bars 9–16   We want small skipping steps so that all can keep together and not have shorter pupils left behind by taller ones.

Bars 17–24   With feet together in the bounces, the distance travelled on each bounce will be small. A bounce and twist combination is good fun and well liked, and cuts down the forward travel distance, helping to keep an excellent circle shape.

Bars 25–32   One hand forward joins the reaching back hand of the pupil to your right, in front of you, in the circle. The teacher sets a sensible length of stepping for the travelling.

Lesson Plan 9 • 25 minutes
January

Theme: *Variety in body parts actions. Variety, like contrast, adds interest for performers and observers.*

Warm-up Activities
4 minutes

1   Stand near a partner for our little dance. I will sing the words and I hope that you will join in quickly, to help me.
    See the little hands go clip, clip, clap, (clap hands)
    Then the feet go trip, trip, trap, (stamp feet)
    I've one word to say to you, (point a finger)
    Come shake hands, how do you do? (partners shake hands)
    Merrily we dance around, just so, (skip around together)
    Then we bow and off we go. (bow, separate and find a new partner)

2   Well done, everybody. It is interesting to see the different hand and feet actions in that little dance. Let's all sing and dance again, and show me how different your actions can be.

Movement Skills Training
15 minutes

1   Sit down in a space with legs bent and feet flat on the floor. Lean back with hands behind to support you. Try little steps on the spot. Step, step, step, step; step, step, step, stop!

2   Still sitting, walk feet forwards for four counts, then back for four. Forwards, 2, 3, 4; back, 2, 3, 4; walk forwards, 3, 4; back, 2, 3 and stop!

3   Jump up to standing. Do little, low jumps from one foot to the other. Jump, 2, 3, 4, foot to foot to foot to foot.

4   Stand with feet apart. Can you swing from side to side, until your body is on one foot only each time with the other foot lifted off the floor (illustrated)? Swing, swing, side to side; 1, 2, 3 and still.

5   Remember where your own space is. Show me lively ways to travel away from and back to your own space. I will beat out eight counts to take you away, and eight counts to bring you back. Ready? Travel, travel, away, away, lively travel, 7, now back; travel back, travel back, 5, 6, home again.

6   Well done. Most of you managed that. Let's have one more practice and remember to do lively skipping or running or bouncing.

Dance — Clever Feet
6 minutes

1   We'll call our dance 'Clever Feet' as we join together the actions we have just practised. All sit down and... step on the spot, 3, 4; again on the spot, 3, 4; walk forwards, 3, 4; walk back, 3, 4.

2   Jump up and show me your low jumps from foot to foot. Jump, 2, 3, 4, foot to foot, 3, 4. Swing, swing, side to side; 1, 2, 3 and still.

3   Now the hardest part – travel away for eight counts, then back to your place for eight. Go!

4   That was excellent. The sitting, the standing, the travelling and your very 'Clever Feet' made it interesting to look at.

5   Let's try to be clever and do the dance straight through without stopping. Begin!

6   Half will now watch half to enjoy watching some of the many actions our clever feet can do.

Dance

Teaching notes and NC guidance
Development over 2 lessons

'Variety' can refer to a mixture of different actions being practised and improved, or a range of ways that one action can be performed. Variety is interesting and worthwhile for its own sake, and eventually is the biggest contributor to the class repertoire.

Improvement with the emphasis on variety is inspired by:

a direct teaching of specific skills by the teacher, as in the opening song

b direct teaching of specific actions, as in the middle third of the lesson

c indirect, shared choice teaching, as in the middle third of the lesson and the 'Clever Feet' dance, where pupils are challenged to plan 'lively ways to travel away from and back to your own space' – in shared choice teaching, the teacher decides the nature of the activity (travelling), and the pupils decide the actions

d observing others demonstrating and then discussing any actions that pupils thought were special, worth remembering, worth copying – and, of course, worth praising.

Warm-up Activities

1 For the very first practice, the teacher, with a partner, can sing each line and show the accompanying action, then do it a second time with the whole class joining in.

2 We want whole-hearted, larger than life actions that will emphasise the variety within them. Big everything, please!

Movement Skills Training

1 Seated, bent-leg stepping on the spot, feeling and hearing the 1, 2, 3, 4 repeating rhythm, is an enjoyable whole-class activity and an excellent exercise for the abdominal muscles.

2 If the steps forwards and back are done with tiny steps, they can be performed with the flat foot pressing down on the floor.

3 Standing, little, low jumps, side to side, from foot to foot, can be accompanied by the teacher's quiet, rhythmic 'Jump, jump, jump, jump' to encourage gentle, easy jumps.

4 Sideways swinging to lift a foot is an unusual activity. 'Tick, tock, tick, tock' vocal sounds from the teacher will encourage a long, slow, pendulum-type swinging.

5 Pupils need to look at the floor to see if there is a distinguishing line or mark from which they travel and to which they try to return. They might, also, be in line with a piano, door or window. This eight-count pattern is long enough for an interesting journey each way.

6 To improve, pupils are asked to repeat the travelling with even greater vigour.

Clever Feet Dance

The title 'Clever Feet' puts the class 'in the picture' regarding what the lesson is all about. The joined-up, varied, neat and clever actions of feet and legs are made easier with the help of the teacher's rhythmic counting and commentary, keeping the whole class together and reminding them what comes next. 'When you are watching the other half demonstrating, please look out for and tell me about really interesting, neat, clever feet that impress you.'

Lesson Plan 10 • 25 minutes
February

Theme: *Body contact sounds. Making and moving with the sounds.*

Warm-up Activities
4 minutes

1 Show me your favourite ways to travel to all parts of the room, listening to my drum beats. When the drum stops – sometimes suddenly – quickly show me a body shape that is still and without any wobbling. (Teacher continues playing and stopping, using different lengths of time for each action. The rhythm is varied to suggest skipping, marching, pattering, for example.)

2 Well done. You listened and moved really well. Watch this little group and see how they start and stop, exactly with the sounds.

Movement Skills Training
15 minutes

1 Can you make a sound with your hands? Try clapping your hands together for four counts, then slapping your hands against your legs for four. Go! Clap, clap, clap, clap; slap, slap, slap, slap; clap hands, 3, 4; slap legs, 3, 4. (Repeat several times for practice until everyone is feeling the rhythm.)

2 Very quietly, tap the floor gently, using each foot in turn. Tap, tap, tap, tap; tap, 2, 3, 4; change feet, change feet; 1, 2, 3, stop!

3 Now, can you show me four claps and four slaps, all accompanied by your quiet, gentle taps? Ready? Go! Clap and tap, clap and tap; slap and tap, slap and tap; clap and tap; clap, 2, 3, 4; slap, 2, 3, 4. (Repeat.)

4 Show me lively sounding stamps as you travel with firm steps, beating the floor. Stamp, stamp, 3, 4; swing your arms, lift your legs; beat, beat, beat the floor; firmly, firmly, 3, 4.

5 As you stamp forwards this time, can you make body sounds for me? You can clap hands or legs again, or you can make a new kind of sound. You can click fingers, or clap a different body part with a hand (chest, shoulder, forearm; or slap upper arms against your sides). Keep your rhythm going with the drum. Stamp and travel, 3, 4; stamp and sound, 3, 4; strong legs, keep going, keep going.

Dance – Tapping and Stamping
6 minutes

1 The first part of the dance is done in pupils' own space as they tap feet and clap hands, for four counts – tap and clap; tap and clap; tap and clap; tap and clap, stop! Now the combination is to continue tapping feet, but add a handslap against a leg – tap and slap; tap and slap; tap and slap; tap and slap, stop!

2 Praise should always identify the nature of what is good so that all can hear, and be informed, rather than a vague 'That was good.'

3 On the move, pupils are challenged to use stamping travelling and their own choice of body sounds, stamping and big lively sounds, which are a contrast to those gentler ones on the spot.

4 The rhythm for the two part sequence, on the spot and while travelling, and the actions to be presented, are assisted by the teacher's drumming and commentary.

5 When pupils are watching the other half of the class perform, they need to be asked to look out for something that answers the challenge and is worth seeing, remembering, and even copying, and is, of course, a source of great pride to the performers.

Dance

Teaching notes and NC guidance
Development over 2 lessons

Pupils should be taught to use rhythmic responses as they perform basic skills. As they leave the hall after this lesson, one might expect the pupils to be chanting, 'One, two, three, four; one, two, three, four' and stepping in time to their chant, after experiencing so many rhythmic practices led by the teacher and the drum – 'Clap, 2, 3, 4; slap, 2, 3, 4; clap and slap, 3, 4; stamp, stamp, 3, 4'; and so on. Developing rhythmic responses is assisted by:

a listening to and responding to a rhythmic accompaniment such as a drum, often by standing or stepping; counting the four beats out loud and clapping in time with those beats

b listening to and travelling to a rhythmic accompaniment, responding to its stopping and starting, and trying to respond in an appropriate way as the drum suggests marching, skipping, bouncing, sliding or galloping

c making rhythmic sounds with hands or feet to a '1, 2, 3, 4', easy-to-feel, repeating beat

d the teacher rhythmically accompanying the descriptions of the various actions, to help with the rhythm and to be a reminder of what is happening. 'On the spot, clap and tap; on the spot, slap and tap; travel and stamp, lively sounds; stamp and stamp, noisy stamps.'

Warm-up Activities

1 Activities used for warm-ups also aim for an attentive start to the lesson by making the class listen for the variable drum beats, and to respond immediately to the drum stopping.

2 This specific praise is for the listening and the moving, focusing the attention on these during the demonstrations.

Movement Skills Training

1 Being asked, surprisingly, for hands sounding and slapping, continues to hold pupils' attention, as does the rhythm being set by the teacher.

2 The 'body parts sounds' emphasis of the lesson means that we want to hear the tapping.

3 Now, the linking of claps and slaps with the taps is an exercise in 'linking actions thoughtfully', which is a recurring NC requirement throughout Physical Education.

4 Showing contrast is an ever-present feature of improvements in Dance. Here, the contrast is between on-the-spot movement and travelling.

5 To the sounds of feet travelling, we now add in additional body contact sounds.

Tapping and Stamping Dance

1 It is worth reminding the class, 'We can accompany Dance with music, percussion, vocal sounds and with body parts contact sounds as in this lesson. Make good sounds, please.'

2 Once again, the teacher's praise is specific, explaining his or her pleasure at the good sounds, good rhythm and particularly good taps. The need to be specific with praise means that the teacher always has to be a really good observer of what is being done well.

3, 4 The teacher's 'rhythmicising' reminds pupils of the actions and the appropriate speeds.

5 The half-watch-half demonstrations need a focus if they are to bring about an eventual improvement. 'Look out for and tell me about good actions, good sounds, good rhythm.'

Lesson Plan 11 • 25 minutes
February

CD TRACK 9

Theme: *Body contact sounds and rhythms.*

Warm-up Activities
4 minutes

Show me that you can 'feel' the rhythm of this lively country dance music by standing, tapping and clapping for eight counts; dancing away from me for eight counts; dancing back towards me for eight counts; then standing and stamping your feet for eight counts. Go! Stand and tap, stand and clap, 5, 6, now go away; dance away, 3, 4, travel, travel, stand and stamp; lift your knees, stamp, stamp, 5, 6, start again.

Movement Skills Training
15 minutes

1 All sit down and see if you recognise the nursery rhyme I am sounding on the floor with my hands and feet. Do not shout out the answer, please.

2 *'Humpty Dumpty sat on a wall'* sounded with both hands; *'Humpty Dumpty had a great fall'* sounded with soles of feet; *'All the king's horses and all the king's men'* sounded with hands on the floor; *'Couldn't put Humpty together again.'*

3 When pupils identify the nursery rhyme, they remain seated and accompany the teacher in sounding it out on the floor, making their own sounds with hands and feet, and saying the words.

4 All stand and say the first line, making hand-clapping sounds: *'Humpty Dumpty sat on a wall.'* You can tap if you like.

5 For the second line, dance and skip, making strong sounds with your feet, on the spot: *'Humpty Dumpty had a great fall.'*

6 For the third line, stand, clapping: *'All the king's horses and all the king's men.'* Tap, if you wish.

7 For the last line, dance about, making sounds with both hands and feet. *'Couldn't put Humpty together again.'*

8 Let's practise all four lines without stopping and let me hear your rhythms and your words loud and clear.

Dance — Humpty Dumpty
6 minutes

1 Find a partner and decide who is number one and who is number two.

2 Line one. Number one dances on the spot, making feet and hand-clapping sounds while number two dances, circling around number one, also making feet and hand-clapping sounds: *'Humpty Dumpty sat on a wall.'*

3 Line two. Change over and repeat, as for line one: *'Humpty Dumpty had a great fall.'*

4 Line three. Pupils stand facing each other and carefully clap hands together to make the rhythm: *'All the king's horses and all the king's men.'*

5 For line four, partners stand side by side, facing opposite ways and leaning forwards to beat out the rhythm, very gently, on their partner's back: *'Couldn't put Humpty together again.'*

6 During our next practice, try to keep both feet and hands working, without stopping.

Development can be through partners planning their own short body-rhythms dance to a different nursery rhyme. Pairs can perform for other pairs to see if they recognise the new nursery rhyme.

Dance

Teaching notes and NC guidance
Development over 2 lessons

Pupils should be able to improve performance, through practice, alone and with a partner.

The individual practice in the middle of the lesson is led by the teacher, who sets the rhythm and says the words of each line. The first and third lines can be accompanied with a hand-clap only, or, with a responsive class, a hand-clap and a tapping of feet. Lines two and four are ideally accompanied by lively clapping and dancing on the spot, aiming to produce a strong and audible body sound accompaniment. Lines two and four are helped by a turning and circling to give the feet a little travelling to do.

When several practices have produced an obvious improvement, all take a partner to practise the partner version. Both partners should work non-stop, saying the words and accompanying them with hand and foot sounds for two lines, one on the spot, one circling; then facing to clap on line three; and, finally, gently sounding the rhythm on each other's back on line four.

Once pupils are well-practised, they can be asked, 'As I quietly say the words of the nursery rhyme, can you make clear body sounds to keep with me? If I close my eyes and say the words, would I feel and hear that you are accompanying me throughout? Then I will ask for volunteers to show the class their excellent actions and sound-making.'

Warm-up Activities

Most English and Scottish country-dance music has 32-bar phrasing, broken down into four sets of eight counts, which are easily distinguished. This 4 × 8-count repeating pattern warm-up is helped by the music and by the teacher's calling out of the actions.

Movement Skills Training

1 All pupils sit, listening and looking, in a space from which they can see (and hear) the teacher.

2, 3 Still seated, after the recognition of the nursery rhyme, they slowly say the words and copy the actions of the teacher.

4, 5 Making sounds with the hands is easy. Making the sounds rhythmically with the feet is not so easy. A demonstration by the teacher to show how to do it will be helpful.

6 Pupils should all be experts in hand-clapping after the previous lesson.

7 Because feet make little sound, this will be mainly a hands-sounding practice.

8 Even if the foot sounds are slight, we can still ask for 'loud, clear words'.

Humpty Dumpty Dance

1 Being in a good space in the room, with partners spaced far enough apart to move freely, is an essential start prior to this light-hearted, good fun dance.

2, 3 The circling partner has less than 3 seconds for travelling, and needs to make his or her circle quite small and not wander off.

4 Clapping quickly lets pupils make eight brisk, little hand-claps.

5, 6 A demonstration of the last line by good couples improves this quite tricky movement.

Lesson Plan 12 • 30 minutes
March

Theme: *Linking actions together in a controlled way. We want pupils to be aware of the actions, body parts, shapes and rhythms in these 'joined-up' sequences.*

Warm-up Activities
5 minutes

1 Walk, 2, 3, 4 with low hand-claps; four steps turning on the spot with high hand-claps; four steps walking back to starting places with low hand-claps; four steps turning with high hand-claps. Step and clap, step and clap; turn and clap, turn and clap; step and clap low, step and clap low; turn and clap high, turn and clap high.

2 This time, let your walking steps be low and soft like your low, quiet hand-claps. Let your turning steps be high and strong with high, strong hand-claps. Quietly forwards, 3, 4; turn strongly, 3, 4; forwards, softly, 3, 4; stamp and turn, stamp and turn. Keep going.

Movement Skills Training
15 minutes

1 Like a bubble, can you float gently with your arms lifting high? Lift and float high... turn, slowly and smoothly... sink...

2 Practise joining the parts smoothly. Float high in the air without a sound... turn in the air, slowly around... sink and lower, bending towards the floor.

3 Run, jump, land and be still, floppy like a rag doll. Keep it short and show me your floppy, still finishing shape. Run.... jump... land... and hold still, all loose and floppy.

4 Change from floppy to tall, ready to go again. Run, jump, land and be still.

Dance — Joined-up Actions
10 minutes

1 Stand beside a partner, facing different directions for our 'Joined-up Actions' dance.

2 Keep in time with the rhythm of the tambourine. Both partners will do the four quiet steps away from each other, with low hand-claps; four strong stops turning with high hand-claps; four steps back towards partner, clapping low; and four lively steps, turning, with high hand-claps. Go!

3 Let's have another practice. Look at the floor to see where your starting place is – and try to be exactly there when you come together again. Ready... step and clap, step and clap; turn and clap, turn and clap; back to partner, 3, 4; turning, turning, 3, 4.

4 We kept together there because of the tambourine. Let's now change to moving like a bubble, and I would like three of you to keep the rhythm by saying, 'Floating'; 'Turning'; 'Sinking.'

5 Sarah first, please. 'Floating.' Slowly, gently, up on tiptoes.

6 Now Daniel, please. 'Turning.' Smoothly, one way, then the other.

7 Now Sophie, please. 'Sinking.' Lowering, very slowly, bending.

8 Well done, dancers and speakers. You all worked hard to make it look smooth, neat and 'together'.

9 Now we can join the two very different parts together for interesting variety. Steps and claps, moving apart, then together. Then moving like bubbles, anywhere in the room.

10 In the next practice, feel what your hands and feet are doing in the stepping/clapping. Then feel inside your whole body as it floats, turns and sinks.

11 Half will now perform for the other half to watch and enjoy.

Dance

Teaching notes and NC guidance
Development over 3 lessons

Pupils should be able to show control in linking actions together. Planning and performing joined-up actions neatly, with variety and contrast, is the mark of a good dancer or gymnast.

Successful control in linking actions together is assisted by:

a the teacher continually challenging the class to perform a series of actions, and repeat them, even in the warm-up part of the lesson with its 'Walk, walk, clapping low; turn, turn, clapping high; back to places, clapping low; turn, clap high, turn, clap high'

b the use of imagery in a series of linked actions helps to give the flowing sequence interesting variety and contrast, as when the bubble 'floats... turns... sinks'

c the teacher's vocal rhythmic accompaniment of the groups of actions to keep them flowing one after the other at the appropriate speed, and to ensure that actions are changed

d reminding pupils that we make 'movement' by changing and joining up actions in the same way that we join words to make sentences or join notes to make music.

Warm-up Activities

1 This near-instant start is inspired by the teacher's accompanying rhythmic chanting. 'Walking forwards; turning steps; walking back; turning steps, in groups of four counts with low and high hand-claps – begin! Walk, walk, clapping low; turn, turn, clapping high; walk, walk, clapping low; turn , turn, clapping high.' This simple a; b; a; b sequence, with first and third, and second and fourth actions being repeated, is a good start to the lesson because it is lively, keeps the pupils' attention and has variety, both on-the-spot and on-the-move.

2 Having established the sequence, the teacher now improves it by asking for better quality, better controlled steps with varied use of effort and space, 'low and soft, high and strong'.

Movement Skills Training

1 The immediate use of imagery – floating like a bubble – establishes the hovering, slow rise, turn, and fall quality wanted.

2 Floating with a rising, hovering, lightly on tiptoes start; turning, slow, gentle, smooth middle; and a very slow, sinking, lowering finish, neatly joined together.

3, 4 The run, jump, land has variety within itself, with the tall, vigorous run and jump contrasting with the soft, squashy landing and floppy finish.

Joined-up Actions Dance

1 In starting places, partners need space to travel without impeding or being impeded.

2 The a; b; a; b repeating sequence is accompanied by the tambourine and the teacher's commentary: 'Step, 2, 3, low claps; turn, 2, 3, high claps.'

3 The 'repeating' sequence is now being intentionally repeated in the same place each time.

4–8 The floating, turning, sinking bubbles parts are introduced by pupil reminders.

9 The two well-practised, contrasting parts of the dance are now being linked together.

10, 11 A feeling for, and an awareness of, what hands and feet do in the stepping and the floating is the 'linking actions thoughtfully' climax of this dance.

Year R

Lesson Plan 13 • 25 minutes
April

CD TRACK 8

Theme: *Simple, traditional-style dance steps and figures.*

Warm-up Activities
5 minutes

1 Skip by yourself, 'feeling' the eight-count pattern of this folk-dance music. Can you change direction as you start a new count of eight? Skip, 2, 3, 4, 5, 6, change direction; travel, 2, 3, 4, 5, 6, change again.

2 This time, skip quietly for six counts, then gently touch hands with someone coming towards you on '7' and '8'. Skip, 2, 3, 4, 5, 6, touch hands, touch hands. Skip, 2, 3, 4, 5, 6, meet and clap.

Teach Steps and Figures of the Lesson's Folk Dance
14 minutes

1 Find a partner and stand side by side, holding hands, in a big circle where you can all see me.

2 In 'advance and retire' we all skip forwards into the circle for four counts, then come out backwards for four counts. Ready... forwards, 2, 3, 4; backwards, 2, 3 and stop. Two or three times without stopping, go!

3 In a chasse step, we face our partner, joining both hands, and step–close sideways, starting with the foot nearer the centre. Ready... step–close, step–close, 3 and out again; step–close, step–close, step–close and stop.

4 Very well done. That is quite difficult. One more practice. Small steps, go!

5 All couples now stand side by side for promenade, hands joined in an anti-clockwise circle. Keep in our big circle for our walk around in this direction. Go! Walk, 2, 3, 4, 5, 6, 7 and stop.

6 We need one more practice, just to get it perfect. Go!

7 Well done. We are all back in our starting places. Now give your partner both hands, and turn each other one way for four counts, then back the other way for four counts. Two hands turn, 3, 4; back again, 3, 4.

Dance – The Muffin Man (English folk dance)
6 minutes

Music – *The Muffin Man* or any 32-bar jig

Formation – big circle with partners

Bars 1–8: All dance to the centre and back.

Bars 9–16: Face partner, taking both of his or her hands and perform four chasse steps to the centre and back.

Bars 17–24: Promenade partners in an anti-clockwise direction.

Bars 25–32: Turn partners, four counts to one side, four counts back again (illustrated).

Keep repeating.

Dance

Teaching notes and NC guidance
Development over 3 lessons

'Pupils should be taught to perform movements or patterns, including some from different times and cultures.'

The 'showing control in linking actions' emphasis of the previous lesson is repeated here.

Linking a series of actions together is an ever-present feature of folk dances, whether they are well-known existing dances or simple, traditional-style dances created by the teacher and used to teach beginners some of the steps and patterns of traditional dance.

A four-part repeating pattern, with each part using eight bars of music of a 32-bar dance, is the most commonly used. For beginners to traditional dance the rhythm is quite quick and will have been practised and 'felt' in the warming-up activities.

Rhythmic accompaniment of the actions by the teacher is the best aid to learning to keep the rhythm: 'Skip, 2, 3, 4, 5, 6, change direction; travel, travel, 3, 4, 5, 6, change again.'

In learning the traditional dance of this lesson, the pupils can be carried along in time with the music, and reminded of the actions by the teacher's chanting of the instructions as he or she joins the class in performing them: 'Skip to the centre, 3, 4; skip back out again; chasse in, both hands joined; chasse back out again; side by side, we promenade round, 5, 6, 7, now turn; turn your partner, 3, 4, back, back, 7, 8 (keep repeating).'

Warm-up Activities

1 This instant warm-up to slowish country dance music is good for gaining attention at the start of the lesson, as it is lively and pupils have to concentrate on 'feeling' and keeping with the eight-count rhythm, as well as on deciding how and where to change direction.

2 Skipping for 6, and touching hands on 7 and 8, is a great favourite and a good challenge if you are to find someone and be near them at just the right times.

Teach Steps and Figures of the Lesson's Folk Dance

Throughout the practising of this four-part dance, each of whose parts takes eight bars of music, the teacher will emphasise 'Keep with the music and use eight counts for each part. Do not be back too early, or, worse still, too late. We never stop dancing because we finish one part just in time to start the next part.'

1, 2 Hands, with arms almost straight, are held out from the sides for the 'advance and retire' start to give everyone room and not be impeded by the person next to you.

3, 4 In the chasse sideways steps, the hand-hold is at about waist height of the shorter partner for comfort, with arms bent.

5, 6 In the promenade, anti-clockwise circle, nearer hands are joined at waist height of shorter partner, and the teacher emphasises, 'Keep our circle round, please.'

7 The two-handed grip for the complete turn around one way, (clockwise first), and back the other, anti-clockwise, way, is with bent arms and hands at just above waist height of the shorter dancer.

Lesson Plan 14 • 30 minutes
May

Theme: *Spring and growth.*

Warm-up Activities
5 minutes

1 Kneel down, curled very small. Stay kneeling, but let me see you start to grow. Unroll your back, shoulders and head, then your arms.

2 Once again, kneel and curl up small, arms and head tucked in. Slowly, start to rise, bit by bit, and finish kneeling tall.

Spring Poem and Movement Skills Practice
16 minutes

1 Children, listen to this spring poem, which is called *The Seed*:
In the heart of a seed, buried so deep,
A dear little plant lay fast asleep,
'Wake', said the sunshine, 'creep to the light',
'Wake', said the voice of the raindrops bright,
The little plant heard and rose to see,
How wonderful the outside world could be.

2 Curl up small, like a seed in the soil. I will read the poem. Show me how a seed can grow.

3 This time, show me which part you are moving first as you start to grow. Head? Shoulders? Back? Elbow? Hand?

4 Decide this time if you want to stay kneeling, or if you are coming right up to standing.

5 Our seed has grown and is looking at what it can see in springtime in our wonderful world.

6 Curl up small again and we'll try to show how a chicken pushes out from its egg, walks unsteadily and then steadily as it becomes stronger. Slowly, push against the inside of your egg. You can use hand, elbow, shoulder, foot, knee, head or back. Please show me.

7 Now stand and show me how unsteady you might be for the first few wobbly steps – with some falling down included. Up and down.

8 Now you can run, jump and make a tiny flight.

9 Well done. Curl up small again and think about how a baby kitten might move soon after it is born. Keep curled, and roll on your back from side to side. Curl and roll, curl and roll.

10 Lie on one side and do a big stretch. Curl and roll on to your other side and stretch again. Curl, roll over, big stretch; curl, roll over, big stretch. Well done. Good curls and stretches.

11 Jump up and land silently. Run, jump, turn and land silently. Run, jump with a turn and land silently. Curl up small and rest.

Dance — Spring Dance
9 minutes

1 For our dance, I will read out the seeds poem and your movements will accompany me. Then we will all show the movements of the very new, unsteady chicken and the curling, stretching, jumping kitten.

2 Feel your whole-body movements this time as you grow; as you push out from your egg; as you do huge bends, stretches and rolls.

3 Practise; improve; remember; perform and observe; make comments.

Dance

Teaching notes and NC guidance
Development over 3 lessons

'Pupils should be taught to express and communicate ideas and feelings, responding imaginatively.'

In Dance, feelings are always expressed through bodily movement. It is hoped that a class will be inspired to express inner feelings of pleasure, excitement, concentration, enthusiasm, etc. through their movement. If a mountaineer can claim to feel 'life effervescing within me' while on his beloved mountains, many young dancers can equally experience intense physical satisfaction.

The feeling we are seeking here is wonderment at springtime growth and new arrivals coming into the world. The purely physical feelings of parts stirring, pushing, appearing and growing are accompanied by feelings of coming alive, of 'being', of release and wanting to have a first look at what the world is like.

There is wonderment at nature as the tiny plant, the chicken and the kitten all manage, unaided, to come alive. The clever plant looks up at the sun; the clever chicken manages, after initial wobbling, to walk, run, jump and do a short flight; the clever kitten learns to do many body movements as well as running, jumping and landing beautifully and softly. Nature is wonderful.

Warm-up Activities

1, 2 We gradually unroll from the bottom part upwards – lower back, shoulders, head, arms.

3 The challenge: 'You choose' invites, possibly, one side of the body to go first, twisting and rising, for example leading with an arm, elbow or one shoulder.

Spring Poem and Movement Skills Practice

1 An awakening, creeping, rising, full of wonder, seed and plant are here being imagined and expressed.

2–5 In this 'shared choice' teaching, the teacher decides the action – growing – and the class decide the actual manner of growth, leading to much use of imagination and variety.

6–11 Growing 'like a chicken coming out of its egg' and 'like the first movements of a baby kitten' uses imagery and imagination, and helps teachers to communicate what we want.

Spring Dance

1 The three-part sequence, moving in the manner of the plant, the chicken and the kitten, emphasises actions first. In what order of body-part actions does the seed grow? Which body parts are pushing open the egg? How do you show the first, unsteady steps of the chicken? Can you curl, roll, stretch, jump and land like the playful kitten?

2 In the next practice, the emphasis is on the effort used as a gently growing plant; as a strong chicken, breaking out of the egg; and as a kitten, firmly curling, rolling, running, jumping and landing.

3 Demonstrations by individuals focus on good body-parts awareness, expressing the identity of seed, chicken and kitten. Originality in expressing ideas through movement should be well praised. With half watching the other half, pupils can be asked, 'Please look out for and then tell me about excellent body movements in the three parts that looked really like the spring time movements we are trying to show.'

Lesson Plan 15 • 30 minutes
June

Theme: *Fast and slow movements as one example of interesting and sometimes exciting contrasts.*

Warm-up Activities
5 minutes

1 Remind yourselves of some of the ways you can travel to a lively piece of music. Show me your best travelling. Go!

2 Hands up all those who were skipping... running... walking... bouncing... hopping... pattering... sliding, etc.

3 Clap with me to the music and feel how easy it is to do groups of four claps. 1, 2, 3, 4; clap, clap, clap, clap; 1, 2, 3, 4; 1, 2, 3, 4, stop!

4 Travel any way you like for four counts, then stay in your space and do four movements (e.g. steps; knee bounces; jumps; bounces; turns; hand-claps; whole-body shakes). Travel, 2, 3, 4; stay and move, 3, 4; off you go, 3, 4; on the spot, 3, 4. (Repeat, several times.)

Movement Skills Training
15 minutes

1 Stand in your own big space and show me a shape that tells me how you are going to move suddenly and very fast. Get ready. Go, go, go, fast; quick, 2, 3, 4; rush, rush, rush, be still!

2 Travel again, fast, using all your muscles – go! Quick, quick, quick, quick; go, go, go, go; 1, 2, 3, fast; quick, quick, quick, stop!

3 Try your fastest possible movements in your own space this time. Move, move, move, fast; quick, quick, 3, 4; 1, 2, 3 and stop!

4 That was very fast, tiring and hard work. Now show me how slowly you can travel. Start in a shape that tells me what you will be doing. This will be your slowest-ever moving. Begin.

5 That was v-e-e-ry s-s-l-ow! Well done, everybody. You can change level if you wish and r-o-ll or cr-aw-l, as well as your slow travel on your feet. Ready... slowest-ever... go.

6 In your own space, perform slow movements using your whole body in bends, stretches and twists as well as slow-motion steps, knee bends and stretches, on the spot.

Dance – Fast and Slow
10 minutes

1 Surprise me with your sudden, fastest-ever and slowest-ever movements. You can travel or perform in your own floor space. Go!

2 You decide when to change from high speed to almost no speed. We should have an exciting mixture of speeds happening together as you change speeds at different times.

3 Your dance will be more interesting if you do: fast moves, travelling; slow moves on-the-spot; fast moves on-the-spot; slow moves travelling, for example.

4 Find a partner and number yourselves one and two. Number one will dance and number two will watch to look out for any special ideas that can be shared with the rest of us. Number ones, begin.

5 Thank you, number ones. Number twos, do any of you want to tell us about something you particularly liked in your partner's 'Fast and Slow' dance? (Comments; observations; further comments; and thanks.)

6 Change places, please. And let's have number twos ready to show off their dance. Number ones, watch your partner's actions and good ideas to share with us.

7 Further practice allows good ideas to be used by everyone.

Dance

Teaching notes and NC guidance
Development over 3 lessons

'Pupils should be taught to develop control and balance in the basic actions of travelling, jumping, turning and stillness.'

The 'control' referred to here is speed control, to show high speed or slow motion and travelling actions from place to place, cleverly adapting the size of the steps to keep balanced and in control of the whole body.

Ultra-high speed and slow motion whole-body movements on-the-spot include actions such as bending, stretching, twisting, turning and arching, and leg actions that can be performed on-the-spot, such as jumping, running, bouncing and stepping.

Bursts of fast travelling or body movements on-the-spot should be short because they are so intense, 'using all your muscles'. Ultra-slow travelling can be performed at floor level, with log rolling by a stretched body, or sideways rolling with a curled-up body. Ultra-slow movements on-the-spot will invite reaching out to all the spaces around you, to the front, sides, high above and behind as well as pulling back into oneself, bending and stretching legs and spine. A good test of pupils' control is for the teacher to call 'Stop!' suddenly and see how quickly they 'freeze' into stillness.

Warm-up Activities

1 This easy, instant start to the lesson asks pupils for their own choice of travelling from their big repertoire.

2 This question also acts as a reminder of the big, interesting variety within the class.

3 Rhythmic clapping to lively music is always a favourite activity, ensuring good attention.

4 A two-part, a; b; a; b repeating sequence of four-count travelling and four-count actions on-the-spot, should include a huge variety of responses which the teacher can praise as pupils are dancing, to expand their ideas.

Movement Skills Training

1, 2 Showing the shape for the intended sudden travel puts pupils in the correct body position for their dash, rush, scatter, high-speed start. 'The floor is hot! Move to a new spot!'

3 Whole body, high-speed moves in own floor space need arms, shoulders, trunk and legs all to make quick, piston-like, in-and-out, up-and-down movements.

4 The starting shape for pupils' slowest-ever travel can be up on tiptoes, ready for tiny steps.

5 Slow travel on hands and knees, or lying down, will be surprise suggestions.

6 On-the-spot, slow-motion movement needs the whole body to rise and fall, bend and stretch, twist and turn, with lots of knee, ankle, hip, spine, arm and shoulder actions.

Fast and Slow Dance

1–3 The teacher's challenge to a class is often 'Can you...?' or 'Can you show me...?' Here the challenge is 'Surprise me...', asking for an extra-special, brilliantly original response and a mixture of speeds on-the-spot and on the move.

4–7 Demonstrations where partner watches partner can be followed by the teacher asking, 'Who thought their partner's "Fast and Slow" dance had brilliant contrasts between the really fast and the very slow? What great ideas did you see?'

Lesson Plan 16 • 30 minutes
July

Theme: *Summer holidays.*

Warm-up Activities
4 minutes

Stand in a circle, hands joined, able to see the teacher who sings and leads the big actions:
Let's join hands in one big ring,
Let's join hands and let us sing,
Let's join hands, both high and low, (reaching up and down)
Let's drop hands and wave 'Hello!' (repeat, with all singing)

Movement Skills Training
16 minutes

1   Listen to this music. It is called *Those Magnificent Men In Their Flying Machines*. Their aeroplanes were small, but they could turn, go up and down, slow down and speed up.

2   All get ready for take-off in your own little magnificent machine. Show me your beautifully stretched wings. Go!

3   Fly to every part of the room, weaving in and out of other aeroplanes. Keep your streamlined shape and let me see you leaning to one side as you do a sharp turn.

4   Well done. I saw some excellent weaving in and out, skimming past lots of other wing tips.

5   When I stop you next time, you will show me with your movements some of the things that might be happening down below you. Flying with lots of gliding and soaring, go!

6   Stop! Show me what might be happening at the seaside (swimming, floating, paddling, rowing, diving, building a sandcastle).

7   That was a good mixture. Well done. Now we fly again.

8   Stop! Show me what big, lively actions can happen in a children's playground (climbing frames, swinging, see-saw, skipping, throwing and catching, cycling, jogging).

9   What a brilliant playground with something interesting for everyone. That was very good. Back to flying again.

10 Stop! We are over a big zoo now. Please show me with your actions and body shapes which animals are in the zoo (monkeys, elephants, penguins, dolphins, seals).

Dance – Summer Holidays
10 minutes

Music: From *Salute to Heroes* by Central Band of the R.A.F.

1   Let's put all the parts of our 'Summer Holidays' dance together now. Our aeroplanes are like magic carpets taking us to see some of the places children visit during their holidays.

2   All ready for take-off in your magnificent machines! When the music stops I will remind you of where you are. Off you go.

3   Seaside – swimmers, floaters, rowers, divers, sandcastle makers.

4   Flying – show me your gliding, ups and downs and turns.

5   Children's playground – climbing, swinging, skipping, throwing and catching, cycling.

6   Flying – weaving in and out, looking down for the zoo.

7   Zoo – monkeys, elephants, penguins, dolphins, seals.

8   Really well done. I enjoyed seeing all those different holiday actions. Let's have another practice, then show one another.

Dance

Teaching notes and NC guidance
Development over 3 lessons

Warm-up Activities

A circle formation, hands joined, with everyone able to see and copy the teacher, is an excellent way to ensure an instant, attentive start to the lesson. The teacher, alone, can demonstrate each of the line's words and actions to start with, then repeat them with the class joining in.

Movement Skills Training

1   Seated, the class listen to the words and the music with the teacher probably adding, 'For our lesson, of course, it will really be *Those Magnificent Men And Women In Their Flying Machines*.'

2   A still start, all nicely spaced apart, leaning forwards, wings outstretched, some already tilted to one side ready for a corner. 'Show me your strong, wide shape.'

3   As always, pupils are asked to 'Visit every part of the room' to discourage flying around in the usual anti-clockwise circle, common in primary school travelling. 'Don't follow anyone!'

4   It is good to be specific when giving praise, to identify and share good ideas. Weaving and skimming will suddenly become more widespread.

5, 6   Encourage big actions at the seaside. This is a physical activity lesson. (No sunbathing!)

7   'Fly again' always receives an enthusiastic, whole-hearted, whole-room response.

8, 9   In the playground, the forwards and backwards swinging, the up and down see-saw, as well as the skipping, throwing and catching, cycling and jogging, can fill the hall with varied action.

10   Dolphins, penguins, elephants, giraffes and monkeys provide lots of choice for the zoo.

Summer Holidays Dance

Pupils should be taught to perform simple movement patterns. One dictionary defines 'pattern' as an 'arrangement of repeated parts'. Improved performance comes from practising, repeating and remembering a manageable sequence of two, three or four simple actions. Without such repetition, there will be no week-by-week development or improvement.

While *Those Magnificent Men In Their Flying Machines* may zoom around freely, sharing the whole room space, vigorously twisting, turning, weaving and gliding in and out of one another, as soon as pupils are challenged to represent the actions taking place down on the ground we want two things – whole-body, vigorous actions, joined in such a way that they can be remembered, repeated, improved and, of course, enjoyed and demonstrated.

For example, at the seaside: 'Swim forwards, swim forwards; float going backwards.' In the playground: 'Sit still on swing; swing forwards; swing back; swing forwards and back to sitting.' At the zoo: 'Elephants, stand on hind legs (lift head and arms forwards and up high in front, as if standing on rear legs); walk forwards, 3 ,4 (upper body dangling down in front of you). Keep repeating the sequence of joined up actions.'

Games

Introduction to Games for Infant Classes

Individual and team games are part of our national heritage and an essential part of the physical education programme. Skills learned during games lessons lend themselves to being practised away from school, alone or with friends or parents, and are the skills most likely to be used in participating in worthwhile physical and social activities after leaving school – an important, long-term aim in physical education.

Vigorous, whole body activity in the fresh air promotes normal, healthy growth and physical development, stimulating the heart, lungs and big muscle groups, particularly the legs. Games lessons come nearest to demonstrating what we understand by the expression 'children at play' with pupils involved in play-like, exciting, adventurous chasing and dodging as they try to outwit opponents in games and competitive activities. Such close, friendly 'combat' with and against others can help to compensate for the increasingly isolated, over-protected, self-absorbed nature of much of today's childhood.

Games lessons are taught outdoors, in the fresh air, in the playground. For infant classes, the playground 'classroom' can be a netball court, if the school has one, or a painted rectangle, sub-divided into six or eight, 8-10 metre rectangles. A painted rectangle is essential because it:

a contains the whole class in a limited space within which the teacher can see, and be easily seen and heard by, the whole class without straining her or his voice in shouting to be heard over great distances.

b gives the spaces needed for the three activities of the final group practices and games part of the lesson. Each space is normally two adjacent rectangles across the court or one third of the netball court.

c prevents accidents by keeping the class well away from potential hazards such as concrete seats, hutted classrooms, fences or walls, all of which should be several metres outside the games rectangle.

d provides lines which are used in hundreds of ways during the infant years' games programme. Pupils run and jump over; balance on; can be 'safe' on in chasing games; aim at; play new games over; use in limited area 'invent a game or practice' situations; play end to end, two with and two against games; and do side to side relays.

Games will appeal to, and be very popular with the majority of pupils if the pupils are always moving; the games are exciting; nobody is left doing nothing; they are fun to play; there is plenty of action; and if rules prevent quarrels, let the games run smoothly and let everyone have a turn and prevent foul play.

The following monthly lesson plans and accompanying notes aim to provide teachers and schools with a wide variety of material for lesson content, development and progression. Each lesson is repeated three or four times to allow plenty of time for planning, practising, repeating and improving.

The following pages also aim to provide a focus for staffroom togetherness and unity of purpose regarding the programme's aims, content and expectations of standards and levels of achievement.

The Infant School Games Lesson Plan – 30 minutes

Warm-up and Footwork Practices (5 minutes) provide a lively start, put the class in the mood for activity, and aim to improve the quality of the running, jumping, chasing, dodging, marking and changing speed and direction.

Skills Practices (10 minutes) form the middle part of the lesson, ideally with all using the same implement so that teaching applies to everyone. Infant lessons will include:

- **individual practices** which allow maximum opportunity to improve as pupils practise with ball, bean bag, skipping rope, hoop, quoit, bat or racket and ball
- **partner practices** to experience the unpredictable behaviour of a ball, for example at different heights, speeds, angles as it does in a game. In co-operative partner practices, partners help each other to master the skills. In competitive partner practices the challenging nature of games, with the testing of skills and wits, and striving to overcome an adversary, are experienced.

Group Practices and Games (15 minutes) are the climax of the lesson, receiving fifteen minutes to allow five minutes for each of the three activities. This important part of the lesson must be given its full time allocation, even if it means cutting other parts short. One of the three activities will always use the implement and the skills practised in the middle of the lesson.

Organisation of the Group Practices and Games Part of the Lesson

At the start of the school year, the class is divided into three mixed groups. They are trained to go and stand in their own starting rectangle within the grids, or thirds of the netball court, when asked 'Please go to your starting places for group activities.' The three sets of implements to be used will have been placed adjacent to, but outside, the enclosed rectangles where they will be used. Balls, bean bags and skipping ropes, for example, are contained within plastic crates to keep them tidy.

The teacher checks that the numbers in each third are correct. If one group has absentees, some pupils are transferred from another group. Then the teacher says, for example, 'Please collect your rope, ball between two, or bean bag between two for your first activity.' When all are standing ready, implement in hand, or beside a partner, the teacher gives a clear explanation of each activity before saying 'Please begin.' The teacher then circulates round the three group practices, giving reminders of the practices and checking that the spacing apart is satisfactory for good practising, and always within the group's own third of the 'playground classroom'.

During the following three lessons of this lesson's development, group activities start with the instruction 'Please go to your starting group places', easily remembered from the previous lesson. They are asked to collect their first activity implement before being told to begin. The teacher circulates round the three different practices or games, reminding them of the practices and main teaching points, progressing the work, giving praise and occasionally presenting a demonstration.

Games equipment. Schools should ensure they have the following:

- sets of 30 of: small balls, medium balls, large balls, beanbags, skipping ropes, playbats, short tennis rackets
- 10 long, 7m skipping ropes for group skipping and for use as 'nets' for tennis and quoits
- 10 rubber quoits
- 6 large, 20cm foam balls
- 8 marker cones
- 1 x set Kwik cricket
- playground chalk.

A Pattern for Teaching a Games Skill or Practice

Excellent lesson 'pace' is expressed in almost non-stop activity with no bad behaviour stoppages and no 'dead spots' caused by queues, over-long explanations or too many time-consuming demonstrations. The teaching of each of the skills combining to make a games lesson determines the quality of the lesson's pace – a main feature of an excellent physical education lesson.

A typical games lesson with its warm-up and footwork practices, skills practices, and small-sided group practices and games, will have about a dozen skills. Whatever the skill, there is a pattern for teaching it.

1   **Quickly into action**. In a few words, explain the task, and challenge the class to start. 'Can you stand, two big steps apart, and throw and catch the small ball to your partner for a two-handed catch?' If a short demonstration is needed, the teacher can work with a pupil who has been alerted. Class practice should start quickly after the five seconds it took the teacher to make the challenge.

2   **Emphasise the main teaching points, one at a time, while the class is working**. A well-behaved class does not need to be stopped to listen to the next point. 'Hold both hands forward to show your partner where to aim.' 'Watch the ball into your cupped hands.'

3   **Identify and praise good work, while the class is working**. Comments are heard by all; remind the class of key points; and inspire the praised to even greater effort. 'Well done, Sarah and Daniel. You are throwing and catching at the right height and speed, and watching the ball into your hands.'

4   **Teach for individual improvement while class are working**. 'Ben, hold both hands forward to give Charlotte a still target to aim at.' 'Grace and Ali, stand closer. You are too far apart.'

5   **A demonstration can be used**, briefly, to show good quality or an example of what is required. 'Stop everyone, please, and watch how Lucy and Michael let their hands "give" as they receive the ball, to stop it bouncing out again.' Less than twelve seconds later, all resume practising, understanding what 'giving hands' means.

6   **Very occasionally, to avoid taking too much activity time, a short demonstration can be followed by comments**. 'Stop and watch Leroy and Emily. Tell me what makes their throwing and catching so smooth and accurate.' The class watch about six throws and three or four comments are invited. For example, 'They are nicely balanced with one foot forward.' 'Their hands are well forward, to take the ball early, then give, smoothly and gently.'

7   **Thanks are given to performers and those making helpful comments**. Further practice takes place with reminders of the good things seen and commented on.

Progressing a Games Lesson Over 4 or 5 Lessons

Gymnastic activities and dance lessons can begin at a simple level of performing the actions neatly, because they are natural and easy. The challenge for the teacher and class is then to plan and develop movement sequences that link these natural actions together, and refine them by adding 'movement elements' such as changes of speed, direction, shape and tension.

Developing a games lesson is different from the above because the eventual target is the mastery of the specific games skills included in the lesson. Such skills include:

○ good footwork used in stopping, starting, changing direction, chasing after and dodging away from other players

○ sending, receiving and travelling with a ball in invasion, striking/fielding and net games, and controlling other games implements such as skipping ropes, quoits, rackets, hoops and bean bags

○ inventing games with agreed rules in co-operation with a partner or small group. Fairness, safety, lots of action and an understanding of the need for rules are the intended outcomes

○ playing competitive games as individuals, with partners, and in small-sided games

○ understanding the skills and particular roles of players as they attack and defend in the three types of games.

Often the starting point, practising the new skill, is a problem, because controlling the implement is difficult. Balls, bats, hoops, skipping ropes, rackets, quoits and bean bags behave unpredictably and the teacher has to simplify the planned skills to enable pupils to succeed and progress in subsequent lessons. Reception class pupils, for example, might have to walk beside a partner, handing the bean bag to each other, before progressing to throwing and catching. In a junior school, 2 versus 1 throwing and catching practice, the teacher can ask the defending pupil in the middle to be passive, with arms down at sides, not aiming to 'steal' the ball that is being passed, and only keeping between the two passing players to make them move sideways and forwards, into a good space to receive the ball.

The varied skills headings listed, fit neatly into both infant and junior games lessons, with their:

○ footwork practices

○ skills practices, which can include 'invent a game'

○ group practices and small-sided games, which can include 'invent a game' and challenges to suggest ways to improve a game with a new rule, other ways to score, or limits on player movement.

Step by step, revising the previous lesson's work, and introducing only one teaching point at a time, the teacher progresses one of the skills of the lesson, for example:

1   Try the slow overhead pull of the rope as it slides along the ground towards you.

2   Can you travel, running over the sliding rope, one foot after the other? Which is your leading leg?

3   On the spot, try a jump and bounce for each turn of the rope. (Slow '1 and, 2 and' skipping action).

4   Try slow running over the rope. Use a small, turning wrist action with hands out wide at waist height.

5   Skip from space to space. Then show me skipping in each space.

6   On the spot, try the slow double beat and the quicker single beat. Then show me neat, non-stop skipping.

7   Pretend your group is on a stage, all doing your best skipping.

National Curriculum requirements for Games – Key Stage 1: the Main Features

'The Government believes that two hours of physical activity a week, including the National Curriculum for Physical Education and extra-curricular activities, should be an aspiration for all schools. This applies to all key stages.'

Programme of study

Pupils should be taught to:

a   travel with, send and receive a ball and other equipment in different ways

b   develop these skills for simple net, striking/fielding and invasion-type games

c   play simple, competitive net, striking/fielding and invasion-type games that they and others have made, using simple tactics for attacking and defending.

Attainment target

Pupils should be able to demonstrate that they can:

a   select and use skills, actions and ideas appropriately, applying them with co-ordination and control

b   vary, copy, repeat and link skills, actions and ideas in ways that suit the activities

c   talk about differences between own and others' work and suggest ways to improve

d   recognise and describe the changes that happen to the body during exercise.

Main NC headings when considering assessment, progression and expectation

○ **Planning** – in a safe, thoughtful, focused way, thinking ahead to an intended outcome. The set criteria are used and there is evidence of originality and variety.

○ **Performing and improving performance** – pupils work hard, concentrating on the main feature of the task, to present a neat, efficient, poised, confident performance, under control.

○ **Linking actions** – pupils work harder for longer, smoothly and safely, using space sensibly, and able to remember and repeat the whole sequence successfully.

○ **Reflecting and making judgements** to help pupils progress and improve, as they plan again adapting and altering as required, guided by their own and others' comments and judgements.

Reception Games Programme

Pupils should be able to:

Autumn	Spring	Summer
1 Respond quickly to instructions, particularly to 'Stop!'	1 Respond immediately and safely to instructions. Work hard to improve and practise skills.	1 Respond readily, quietly, safely to instructions.
2 Listen to teacher while practising. Try to respond to teaching points being made.	2 Continue practising, almost without stopping, until asked to change to a new activity.	2 Show positive attitude to taking part. 'These lessons are fun, good for you, and exciting.'
3 Share playground safely with others, looking for quiet spaces in all areas of playing area.	3 Run quietly with good lift of knees, heels, arms, upper body.	3 Control body in motion; practise to gain confidence.
4 Stop on signal and change to next instruction. 'On "Stop!" show me a still balance on tiptoes. Stop!'	4 Respond enthusiastically to challenges to try things out and experiment.	4 Experiment with varied implements – ball, hoop, quoit, small playbat.
5 Travel in a variety of ways – walk, run, jump, hop, bounce, skip, gallop.	5 Practise vigorously to keep warm in winter.	5 Use feet well at take-off and landing from long and high jumps.
6 Practise diligently by yourself to learn and remember skills.	6 Practise to improve travelling actions such as run, jump, hop, skip, hopscotch, bounce.	6 Extend variety and quality by listening well to instructions.
7 Experiment with one-handed throws and two-handed catches with beanbags, standing and on the move.	7 Throw beanbag, ball, quoit to different heights and catch – low, medium, high.	7 Use left and right hands to throw small ball up, then catch with two hands, standing and on the move.
8 Practise throw and catch with medium ball, standing and moving.	8 Throw a big ball up, let it bounce, catch with both hands.	8 Throw ball up and forwards, run and catch with both hands.
9 Aim quoit at line or mark, with swing back and forwards of arm.	9 Dodge with good footwork, changing direction and speed.	9 Be versatile with hoop, bat and ball, ball, beanbag and quoit.
10 Co-operate with partner, throwing and catching beanbag, quoit and medium ball, about 1 metre apart.	10 Co-operate with partner in simple throw and catch, 1 metre apart, and while walking side by side.	10 Remain in own third of court during group activities and practices.
11 Practise freely with hoop on ground – jumps, balances; and in one or both hands – skipping, bowling.	11 Send medium ball to partner in a variety of ways – throw, kick, head, bounce, roll.	11 Dodge and mark with enthusiasm and controlled use of space.
12 Practise simple chasing and dodging games very carefully.	12 Link simple actions – throw and catch; run and jump.	12 Follow a leader, using a range of implements, copying actions.
13 Participate whole-heartedly in these outdoor lessons.	13 Show better control over beanbag, ball, quoit, hoop and rope.	13 Make short rally with partner, throwing quoit or beanbag over line or long rope 'net'.
14 Show actions to help others.	14 Observe others and point out features admired.	14 Throw ball or beanbag to partner using good judgement of height and force needed for success.
15 Watch demonstrations and say what was pleasing.		15 Link simple actions – walk, run, jump.
		16 Comment on demonstrations and why they are neat, quiet and correct.

Lesson Plan 1 • 30 minutes
September

Emphasis on: *(a) creating a quiet, industrious atmosphere with quick responses; (b) sharing the space sensibly and safely with others; (c) practising to learn, improve and remember the skills being taught.*

Warm-up and Footwork Practices
4 minutes

1 Show me your best running as you go to all parts of our playground 'classroom'. Visit the ends, the sides, the middle and always keep inside the lines of our pretend classroom.

2 Good running is quiet, and you do not follow anyone.

3 When I call 'Stop!' can you be in a big space, all by yourself?

4 Now run and jump over the lines. When I call 'Stop!' next time, can you run to balance, tall and still, on a line?

Skills Practices: with beanbags
10 minutes

Individual practices

1 Can you throw up with one hand and catch with two hands? Throw your beanbag up to about head height.

2 Now, can you walk, throwing up with two hands and catching with two hands? Watch the beanbag carefully all the time.

3 Aim to land the beanbag on a line or mark on the ground. Pick it up, then aim carefully at another line. Swing your throwing arm forwards and back, then aim and throw.

Partner practices

1 Can you walk, side by side, handing the beanbag to your partner?

2 Stand facing your partner and make gentle little throws to each other. Aim for your partner's outstretched hands.

3 Now can you show me a way in which you and your partner can throw or send the beanbag to each other? (For example, walking, side by side, small throws; place beanbag on top of shoe, kick it to partner; aim to land it on partner's flat hands; walk, balancing it on back of a hand, slide sideways on to partner's flat hand.)

Group Practices
16 minutes

Hoop each
Practise freely, sometimes with the hoop on the ground, sometimes holding or sending it. (For example, balancing on ground; hold, throw, catch; send by bowling.)

Beanbag with a partner
Have three turns each, aiming at a hoop on the ground, then change over. Swing a long, slow arm. Aim high enough for beanbag to 'see' and fly into the hoop.

Medium size ball each
Show me how you can send the ball a little distance, up in the air or to other parts of this group's space. (For example, kick, roll, head, bounce, throw, bat.)

Games

Teaching notes and NC guidance
Development over 4 lessons

Warm-up and Footwork Practices

1 The emphasis is on running within the confines of the outside four lines of the area. Regular stopping of the running to bring wayward children back 'inside the lines, please' starts the development of this important tradition. Inside the lines is contained; pupils can hear the teacher; and they are well clear of dangerous fences, huts, concrete benches, etc.

2 A demonstration by a runner, with heels and knees uplifted, explains 'quiet running'.

3 Not being near others or following others can be practised by a sudden 'Stop!' by the teacher, which should show pupils not near others, all facing different ways, and not in an anti-clockwise circle, common in infant-school running.

4 Running and jumping over lines alternates with a held balance, 'tall and still' on tiptoes on the nearest line, when the teacher calls 'Stop!' (Responding to the signal 'Stop!' immediately is being practised often with this new class to establish an essential standard of listening and responding.)

Skills Practices: with beanbags

Individual practices

1 A teacher demonstration of the one-handed throw to head height at most, and the two-handed catch, can precede the practice.

2 Two hands to two hands has the cupped hands ready all the time. The cup closes around the bag and 'grabs it tight'. Demonstrate with someone who is really watching the bag.

3 A teacher demonstration shows the long arm swinging 'forwards, back, forwards and throw' as the beanbag is aimed to land on one of the many lines or marks on the ground, at a distance of only 3 metres. The bag is picked up and another target is found.

Partner practices

1 After getting pupils into twos, ask one to put his or her beanbag down in the place where they were collected from. The one shared bag is handed into the hand of the partner as they walk side by side, 'still keeping inside my playground classroom, please.'

2 Now they stand a very short distance (1 metre) apart, and aim to put the beanbag into their partner's outstretched hands.

3 The challenge 'Can you show me another way to send the beanbag to your partner?' is accompanied by much teacher commentary of the good things seen, and as a help to the less creative. This practice must be done gently, keeping very close.

Group Practices

Hoop each

Practice with the hoop includes using it on the ground for jumps and balances and holding it for spinning and bowling.

Beanbag with a partner

They 'take turns' at aiming to land the beanbag in the hoop, from about 2 metres away.

Medium size ball each

In sending the ball 'a little distance' we encourage much throwing and catching, bouncing and catching, to keep the ball near. Wild, long-distance kicking and so on must be discouraged.

Lesson Plan 2 • 30 minutes
October

Year R

Emphasis on: *(a) vigorous, whole body movements; (b) developing the habit of near-continuous activity; (c) listening, while practising, and responding well to teaching.*

Warm-up and Footwork Practices
4 minutes

1 Can you run and jump over lines and show me your lively ways of landing, then running on without stopping?

2 Can you try long jumps with a long straight front leg?

3 Try a high jump now with the front knee bent and reaching high.

4 When I call 'Stop!' show me how quickly you can run in to the box whose number I call out. (Teacher has numbered playground rectangles 1, 2, 3.)

Skills Practices: with hoops
10 minutes

Individual practices

1 Put your hoop on the ground, nicely spaced away from others. Now run and jump in and out of all the hoops, without touching them (like stepping stones).

2 Can you run, jump up high, then do a nice, squashy landing into your own hoop?

3 Pick up your hoop and either try spinning it, or walk beside it, bowling it forwards.

Partner practices

1 Show your partner something you like doing with your hoop, on the ground or in your hand. Your partner can either try to copy this or show you their favourite activity.

2 Can you and your partner hold your hoops and face each other, standing inside the hoop? Now try to roll the hoop sideways, still walking on the inside, very slowly and carefully. Can you keep going at the same speed, together?

Group Practices
16 minutes

Partners: beanbag each

Follow the leader, who walks and shows you a simple activity with their beanbag. Following partner watches and tries to copy. (For example, throw and catch; balance on head or back of hand; kick up from toe of shoe; bat up repeatedly.)

Hoop each

Can you do something lively with the hoop on the ground, and something where you hold it in one or both hands? 'Lively' – run and jump; hopscotch around; in hand, twist, throw and catch, bowl; skip with swing overhead (illustrated).

Small size ball each

Can you walk, throwing and catching, and try to do a quick hand-clap between throw and catch? (Clap puts hands into good position for catches, near eyes, in front.) Can you try some one- and two-handed ways of throwing and catching, on the move?

Games

Teaching notes and NC guidance
Development over 4 lessons

Warm-up and Footwork Practices

1   Running and jumping, without stopping, is a great favourite with young children, and the lines give them a focus for their jumps.

2   The long, straight front leg in long jumping through the air can be demonstrated by the teacher or by one of the many children who will be doing this well. In a long jump you can see the foot of the front leg reaching out in front.

3   A high jump to lift you upwards has a bent front knee, reaching up as your arms are doing.

4   Class is shown the different, numbered rectangles and all call out the number of each as they are introduced to it. They should then know where to race when a number is called.

Skills Practices: with hoops

Individual practices

1   After placing own hoop down in a space, pupils run and jump into and out of all the hoops, like playing 'stepping stones'.

2   Now they stop after each run and jump into a hoop to show a 'nice, squashy landing' with a bending of the knees.

3   If bowling is too erratic, let pupils try to spin the hoop on the spot. With both, a teacher demonstration and explanation are essential. To start the bowling, hold the hoop upright at your right side if right handed, with your left hand on top. The bowling hand is placed across the hoop away from you and pulls the hoop forwards to make it roll.

Partner practices

1   The simplest partner work is always to 'Show your partner a favourite activity. Then your partner will demonstrate for you.' This allows the teacher to see the extent of the ability and the success of the teaching that has gone before.

2   The slow, sideways balance walk inside the hoop is another activity that can be controlled and easily practised because both hands are helping. As a mirroring activity, it is good fun and gives pleasure when both manage to keep together.

Group Practices

Partners: beanbag each

The friendly pleasure of partner work is experienced again, with a beanbag each, in 'Follow the leader'. 'Follow' infers going somewhere, so encourage pupils to keep moving – something that will be important anyway as weather becomes colder. Balance on hand or head; throw and catch; and throw/aim to land on a line are all good activities.

Hoop each

Something 'lively' with the hoop means a big body action, either using the hoop on the ground for jumps or skips around; or bowling or skipping vigorously.

Small size ball each

'Throw, clap, catch' using one hand for the throw, and two cupped hands for the catch, should be practised with eyes looking closely at the ball throughout, and with the ball being thrown no higher than head height, particularly when walking as well.

Lesson Plan 3 • 30 minutes
November

Emphasis on: *(a) enjoying the experience of vigorous physical activity; (b) practising whole-heartedly, almost without stopping, to become and stay warm, important as weather becomes colder in winter; (c) receiving and controlling, travelling with, and sending a ball.*

Warm-up and Footwork Practices
4 minutes

1   Show me your good, quiet running, as you visit all parts of our playground 'classroom'. Remember to lift heels and knees, and do not follow anyone.

2   When I call 'Stop!' show me your good running shape with your body leaning slightly forwards, arms bent, and in a good space. (Several practices.)

Skills Practices: with medium-size balls
10 minutes

Individual practices

1   Can you walk, throwing and catching with both hands?

2   Can you throw the ball up in front, let it bounce, then catch it with two hands?

3   Now can you show me another way or ways to send the ball a little distance, collect it, then send it again (e.g. throw, roll, kick, head, bat, bounce)?

Partner practices

1   Walk side by side, handing the ball to each other, practising a good hand position for receiving (i.e. cupped, fingers forwards).

2   Now can you walk, side by side, making a little throw to each other, with your hands ready, showing your partner where to aim?

3   Can you and your partner show me another way or ways that you can send the ball to each other (e.g. throw, bounce, roll, kick, head, bat, run and hand)?

Group Practices
16 minutes

Beanbag each

Walk around inside own space, throwing and catching. As you come to line in front of hoops, aim to throw beanbag into hoop (about 2 metres away). Brisk walk around the rectangle circuit to keep warm. Walk, three or four catches, then aim.

Medium-size ball between two

Send the ball a short distance to your partner (illustrated). Can you keep on the move to keep warm as you kick, head, hand, bounce or throw your ball very carefully and gently. One could stand and other circle around for throw and catch with frequent changes. About 1 metre apart.

Ropes and hoops on ground

Ropes lie straight, curved and in a V-shape. Hoops are scattered around among ropes. Groups can run and jump in and out of hoops like stepping stones. You can jump from side to side over rope, across or along, or over Vs increasing width.

Games

Teaching notes and NC guidance
Development over 4 lessons

Warm-up and Footwork Practices

1 Good running is quiet and you don't run behind or follow anyone. Unless taught otherwise, young children all run in a big anti-clockwise circle, following everyone else. We ask them to 'visit every part of the playground classroom' to discourage the curving, anti-clockwise circle. By running on straight lines into corners, towards ends, sides and through the centre, the quality and variety of the running are greatly enhanced.

2 The slight lean of the whole body into the running, with arms bent to allow a quick arm action to match the leg action, lets the class feel these positions.

Skills Practices: with medium balls

Individual practices

1 From now on, right through the colder winter months, we ask for practising 'on the move' or 'walking' to try to maintain the body heat built up in the warm-up activities. Use both hands for throwing and catching at head height, where your eyes can see the ball well. Praise those who are 'throwing up carefully to head height only' and those who are 'really looking at the ball all the time.'

2 The throw up in front, usually with straight arms, is above head height, sufficient to allow the ball to bounce up to about waist height for the next catch.

3 Emphasise that the sending of the ball must be contained within our playground classroom, within the marked rectangle. Wild kicking or throwing must be stopped and replaced by careful, gentle throws, kicks, headers, bounces, rolls.

Partner practices

1 Side-by-side walking and handing the ball to each other lets pupils practise the correct receiving position of the hands, with fingers spread on the sides, facing forwards.

2 Still walking forwards, the arms swing across you very slowly and gently and the ball is released just ahead of the partner, who should be able to walk into the catch, grabbing the ball with both hands.

3 Other ways of partner sending and receiving, freely practised here, must be limited to 3 metres at most to ensure repetition and some chance of success.

Group Practices

Beanbag each

The brisk walking is done around the inside of the third of the whole area, which should be about 20 m × 10 m, and each corner has a hoop as a target in which to aim to land the beanbag.

Medium-size ball between two

In sending the ball a short distance to a partner, on the move to keep warm, moving well to receive efficiently is as important as good sending.

Ropes and hoops on ground

Ask for interesting rope shapes on the ground to give ideas for lively running and jumping practices.

Lesson Plan 4 • 30 minutes
December

Emphasis on: *(a) warming-up well with lots of vigorous leg activity; (b) chasing and dodging games; (c) almost uninterrupted practising of skills.*

Warm-up and Footwork Practices
5 minutes

1 Jog slowly through the ends of our playground 'classroom', and sprint quickly through the middle, watching carefully for others.

2 In jogging, you are nearly upright with not too much lifting of heels and knees. In sprinting, you lean forwards more and lift arms, heels and knees more.

3 All-against-all 'tag' or 'it', trying not to be touched (caught) but also trying to touch as many others as possible. No hard pushing. Gentle touches only, for safety.

4 'Stop!' Who caught lots of others? Who wasn't caught at all?

Skills Practices: with beanbags or quoits
10 minutes

Individual practices

1 Jog around, making tiny throws and catches, watching beanbag or quoit carefully into your two hands, cupped ready (illustrated).

2 Stand and make a little throw, up and a little way in front of you. Can you run and catch with hands nicely cupped again, and just in front of your eyes (about chest height)? Let your throw be like an aim with a long slow swing of your throwing arm, well up to give you time to get there. Catch with both hands.

Partner practices

1 Use one beanbag or quoit. Jog beside your partner and show me how you give quoit or beanbag to partner, trying not to drop it.

2 Can you stand, facing each other, about 1 metre apart? Use one hand to throw and two hands to catch, with your partner's hands showing you where to aim your careful throw (hands cupped).

3 With a beanbag or quoit each, stand about 3 metres apart (ideally on a line). One of you quietly say 'Ready... aim!' and both will throw, aiming at partner's line, or next to where partner is standing. Then you run to change places, pick up your beanbag or quoit, and the other partner calls 'Ready... aim!'

Group Practices
15 minutes

Small ball each
Can you show me how you can play with ball freely, on the move? (Batting, heading, kicking, bouncing, rolling, throwing.) Keep moving, walking or jogging.

Beanbag or quoit with a partner
Standing about 2 metres apart, can you give each other a long arm-swing aim and throw for a nice high catch? Do four, then sprint to change places.

Hoops 'tag'
Three chasers with bands are allowed to catch you if you are not 'safe' in a hoop. If caught, take a band and start chasing.

Games

Teaching notes and NC guidance
Development over 4 lessons

Warm-up and Footwork Practices

1   In the end-to-end travelling, the class jog in the outside two thirds and sprint through the middle third, watching carefully for other sprinters coming towards them. A 'Keep to the left' might be a good idea if the area is narrow.

2   Jogging is an easy action with an upright body and a little lift of heels or hands, and the steps are short. Sprinting at speed is done with a forwards lean of body weight, a strong lift of heels, knees and hands, and longer strides.

3   In dodging games like 'All-against-all tag', encourage good dodging actions such as direction changes rather than speedy racing away which leads to bumping and accidents.

Skills Practices: with beanbags or quoits

Individual practices

1   The jogging continues, to keep pupils warm, as they throw up with one and catch with two hands. Cupped hands that close around the bag or quoit, and eyes that watch the object closely at all times, are the main points to encourage, look for and praise.

2   From a standing start position, pupils throw the beanbag up and forwards high enough to give them time to run to where the beanbag is coming down to catch it, standing still. The throw is with a long swing up of the throwing arm.

Partner practices

1   Still jogging, side by side, pupils are asked to give or send the beanbag or quoit to partner for an easy receipt, trying hard not to drop it.

2   Standing 2 or 3 metres apart only, a low one-handed swinging action is used to throw beanbag to partner's two cupped and outstretched hands. On receipt, close hands around object and grab it in to yourself.

3   Partners stand apart on the side lines, or nearer if lines are too far apart. 'Ready... aim!' is for both to respond to. Then they run to partner's side (keeping winter-warm) and repeat to starting line with other partner giving the signal.

Group Practices

Small ball each

Free practice with the small ball must be kept within the group's third of the area, and ideally will be practised 'on the move' to keep warm. Teacher commentary on and praise for the varied activities will extend the group's repertoire, as they use hands, feet and head in their varied ways.

Beanbag or quoit with a partner

At 2 metres apart, pupils should be able to succeed often with the long arm swing/aim as they send beanbag or quoit to their partner, who stands with cupped hands, forwards and ready, as a target to aim for. 'Run to change sides to keep warm.'

Hoops 'tag'

Last person caught starts the next game in which all pupils have a coloured band on, except the chaser. When caught, take band off, put it down beside the other bands, and start chasing.

Lesson Plan 5 • 30 minutes
January

Emphasis on: *(a) whole-hearted, safe and almost continuous action to keep warm; (b) developing simple, linked actions; (c) co-operating with a partner to improve and extend skills.*

Warm-up and Footwork Practices
5 minutes

1   Play follow the leader with your partner, and show me some lively running, jumping, hopping, skipping or bouncing actions.

2   Can you copy each other exactly, with your feet doing the same actions at the same time (i.e. mirroring, in unison)?

3   Now play 'tag' or 'it' with your partner (illustrated). In this game, you may only touch your partner when he or she is not on a line (i.e. on a line is safe, untouchable, but regular excursions from the lines are encouraged to keep them moving). Change duties often.

Skills Practices: with a small ball
10 minutes

Individual practices

1   Jog around, holding your ball in cupped hands as if you had just caught it. Keep moving and looking for spaces to run into. When I call 'Change!' place your ball down, still, on the ground, leave it and find another ball to pick up and carry. I will be looking to see how quick you are. 'Change!' (Repeat several times.)

2   Change to walking, throwing and catching with two cupped hands, and fingers pointing forwards. Can you keep a nice rhythm with your little throws, up and slightly in front of you? 'Throw, walk, catch; throw, walk, catch; throw, walk, catch.'

3   If your hands are cold, put them under your armpits and jog around, dribbling the ball like a footballer. Dribble a few times, then stop the ball by putting your foot on top of it.

Partner practices

1   Stand, facing your partner, two big steps apart. Throw with one hand and catch with two at three different heights: a low one below the knees; a medium one to the waist; and a higher one to the chest.

2   Can you plan one or more ways to send the ball carefully to your partner, and keep moving to keep warm? (Side-by-side handing or throwing; football passing; one throwing, one heading; throwing up to let it bounce in front of the other, etc.)

Group Practices
15 minutes

Medium-size ball with a partner

Send the ball to partner through the 2-metre space between beanbags (e.g. kicking, rolling, throwing, batting, heading).

Small ball each

Can you 'juggle' your ball to keep it going up and bouncing? Strike with foot, head, thigh, front and back of hands.

Walking 'free and caught'

Three of group chase the seven others to catch them. When caught, stand still, with hands on head, until 'set free' by someone touching elbows.

Games

Teaching notes and NC guidance
Development over 4 lessons

Warm-up and Footwork Practices

1 Partners could have been organised in the classroom to allow an instant start on arriving in the playground. Minimum waiting and maximum action are the most important aims in mid-winter. Pupils are told to follow the leader at a distance of about 2 metres so that the leader's actions and uses of feet can be seen easily.

2 If they can step, skip, run and jump, bounce, etc. at the same speed, copying step for step in unison, they deserve a special word of praise for effort and skilful observation.

3 Tag against a partner is made more interesting by the rule that you may only catch your partner when he or she is not on a line and 'safe'. When one is caught they change over duties.

Skills Practices: with a small ball

Individual practices

1 Jogging and listening for 'Change!' is an example of an activity designed to develop attentive, quick responses. Ball is placed down gently on playground to prevent it rolling away. A different ball is picked up and the game continues.

2 Aim for a repeating rhythm and successful catching as pupils keep on the move, weaving in and out of one another. Ball is watched closely into hands which close around it to grab it in.

3 Football dribbling, with ball near enough to feet for instant stops, using inside, outside and laces parts of the shoe to stroke the ball forwards or from side to side.

Partner practices

1 Couples stand 2 to 3 metres apart only, with one foot forwards to help them to bend down for the low catches, below the knee. Throw is with a long, straight arm aiming at partner's outstretched and cupped hands.

2 Ball is sent only 2 to 3 metres from partner to partner to contain it in your third of the play area, to reduce time wasted chasing after wayward throws, and to provide the optimum practice time. Emphasise the importance of the receiving, which is helped by moving early to be standing ready in place for the ball.

Group Practices

Medium-size ball with a partner

Partners have to plan how to send the ball through the small space between the two beanbags. The same or different methods may be used. One partner could bounce it through while the other partner could kick it through. If it is very cold, they can 'Do four, then run to change sides to start again.'

Small ball each

In juggling, the ball is struck upwards, then allowed to bounce once, then struck upwards, then allowed to bounce. This is a lively practice because players need to keep moving to get to the ball after each bounce to strike it up again.

Walking 'free and caught'

Three chasers wear bands to identify them. They are told to touch gently without any dangerous pushing. Let games run for about 15 seconds, then change over the chasing trio.

Lesson Plan 6 • 30 minutes
February

Emphasis on: *(a) vigorous, immediate responses to become and stay winter-warm; (b) good footwork – dodging and chasing, and changing directions; (c) enjoying learning to control a big ball.*

Warm-up and Footwork Practices
5 minutes

1 Can you show me some lively ways you can travel to visit all parts of our playground 'classroom'? Are your actions so quiet that I would not hear you if I closed my eyes?

2 Mostly we go forwards but some movements can be done going sideways. Can you think of and show me any (e.g. slipping, skipping, bouncing)?

3 'Free and caught' with a quarter of the class wearing bands as chasers. If caught you stand still with hands on head. Those who are not caught can free you by touching you on the elbow. Changing direction suddenly is a good way to dodge. (Chasers are changed over often with comments on good performances.)

Skills Practices: with a large ball
10 minutes

Individual practices

1 Walk or jog using two hands to throw the ball just above your head. Try to catch it with two hands just in front of your eyes (i.e. ball stays high). Thumbs behind and fingers well spread.

2 Keep walking and bounce the ball down just in front of you with both hands pushing. Catch the ball as it bounces back up.

3 Practise freely with your ball to show me how you can send it and then collect it (e.g. kick, throw, bounce, head, roll). Remember to keep inside the lines of our 'classroom'.

Partner practices

1 Stand facing your partner, about two big steps apart. Can one of you send the ball straight to your partner and the other one send it with a little bounce between you (i.e. chest and bounce passes)? Use both hands each time, aiming carefully.

2 Like rugby players, can you jog side by side, and either throw a gentle, easy pass or hand it carefully to your partner?

3 Have some free practice, sending the ball in a favourite way that seems to work for the two of you.

Group Practices
15 minutes

'Follow the leader' with choice of quoits, beanbags, hoops or balls
'Follow' means going somewhere, moving to keep warm. Leader, do something simple.

Large ball with a partner
Can you invent a simple game? For example, throw for header; aim at line contest; kick to each other; chase to touch ball.

Free practice with rope in one or both hands, or on ground
Try skipping with a slow pull of rope along ground, or run and jump over rope.

Games

Teaching notes and NC guidance
Development over 4 lessons

Warm-up and Footwork Practices

1   The class repertoire of lively leg activities appropriate for warming up the body will include running; running and jumping; skipping; skipping with long, upwards arm swings; bouncing with feet together; slipping steps sideways; and hopping.

2   Tell them that 'forwards' means that the front of our body is going first. When we go 'sideways', one side of our body goes first. 'Backwards' should be done with great care and only for a few steps, while looking behind you over one shoulder.

3   Chasers are told to touch 'gently so that no-one is pushed over and hurt.' Dodgers are encouraged to dodge by using good footwork such as a change of direction, rather than high-speed running away. Change the chasers every 15 seconds or so.

Skills Practices: with a large ball

Individual practices

1   Ball is held in both hands, starting at head height and thrown to just above head height. Pupils are asked to try to catch with both hands just in front of the eyes where ball can be 'seen' right into the hands.

2   Two-handed bouncing to bring the ball up to waist height for an easy two-handed catch should be tried 'on the move' by reaching forwards to bounce it down to come up for you.

3   Ask for 'little' throws, kicks, headers, bounces, rolls, batting to lessen the number of runaway balls.

Partner practices

1   The straight chest pass is aimed at your partner's chest. The bounce pass is aimed just in front of partner's feet.

2   Whether throwing or handing the ball, pupils run almost shoulder to shoulder to make the pass as easy as possible.

3   Free practice at 2 to 3 metres apart is ideally done on the move, so should be something pupils find quite easy.

Group Practices

'Follow the leader' with choice of quoits, beanbags, hoops or balls

On alternate weeks, pupils can be leader and decide the equipment to be used. 'Following' means going somewhere, which we hope means keeping warm, particularly if the activity is simple for the sake of successful repetition. 2 metres apart lets the follower have a good look at the leader's actions.

Large ball with a partner

The 'simple game' which they are challenged to invent for two players with one ball can be a simple practice of a skill or a little 1 v 1 competition, e.g. throw up to self to head it past partner on a line; aim to throw it past partner, guarding a line; run after partner to touch ball held by him or her.

Free practice with rope in one or both hands, or on ground

Skipping rope on ground can be jumped over or bounced along, from side to side or above. A held rope can be used to learn to skip by turning rope overhead to hit ground and slide towards you, for a step over. Skippers are asked to show their best skipping, sometimes on the spot, sometimes on the move.

Year R

Lesson Plan 7 • 30 minutes
March

Emphasis on: *(a) an enthusiastic response to the challenge to try out new activities; (b) varied ways to use a skipping rope; (c) co-operation with a partner.*

Warm-up and Footwork Practices
5 minutes

1   In your running, can you show me a good lifting of knees and heels to make it quiet? Remember to run along straight lines, never following anyone. (Primary school children run in an anti-clockwise circle, following each other, if not taught otherwise.)

2   'Five points tag'. All have five points to start with. All chase and dodge away from all. If 'tagged' by someone, you lose one of your starting five points.

3   'Stop!' Who was a good dodger and kept four or five points? Who was a good chaser and caught more than three others? (Repeat.)

Skills Practices: with skipping ropes
10 minutes

Individual practices

1   Place rope flat and straight on ground. Jump, skip or hop from side to side along and back. Can you make up a little rhythm as you go? 'Jump over, then bounce; jump over, then bounce; hop, 2, 3 and turn.'

2   Make a circle shape on the ground. Can you jump right across, or into and out of, or do a big high jump into it?

3   Pick up your rope and try skipping freely. (Those who cannot skip yet can skip along, rope in one hand at side, turning the rope to hit the ground.)

Partner practices

Jump the wriggling snake. One partner, with rope, crouches down and makes the long rope wriggle up and down in waves on the ground with a strong wrist action. Running and jumping partner crosses rope from both sides. Change over often.

Group Practices
15 minutes

Small ball with partner

Can you and your partner invent a simple little game to practise throwing and catching?

Skipping rope each

Practise freely, trying to skip on the move, pulling the rope slowly over to slide towards you to step over it (illustrated), if just learning. (Better ones, on the spot and moving.)

Partners: one hoop and five beanbags

Each has five aims to land the beanbags in the hoop, from a line about 3 metres away. What is your best score out of ten?

Games

Teaching notes and NC guidance
Development over 4 lessons

Warm-up and Footwork Practices

1   Short bursts of flat-footed, noisy running, followed by running on tiptoes with a good feeling of lifting heels and knees, will let the class hear what is and what is not wanted. By now the running should be well-established as straight-line running, never circling or following others, with visits to all parts of the teaching space.

2   Depending on the class subtraction ability level, the five points from which they subtract one each time they are caught (i.e. touched gently by another) may need to be changed to four or three.

3   Stop the game after 15 seconds to calm pupils down and check on 'Who is a good dodger and still has five points? Who is a good chaser and caught three or more?'

Skills Practices: with skipping ropes

Individual practices

1   Ropes are well spaced out, lying straight on the ground. Lively, end-to-end skipping, jumping, hopping or bouncing is helped by a feeling of rhythm within the short sequence.

2   A circle shape challenges pupils to leap across or to run, jump and land inside. 'Which is your jumping-off foot? Can you jump up from two feet sometimes? Can you do a nice, squashy landing?'

3   Trying to skip can be the real thing with overhead pulls of the rope, or simply running with the rope at one side in one hand, which turns the rope in a circle as you run along.

Partner practices

The wriggling snake, waving up and down in ripples just above ground level, is unpredictable with interesting highs and lows to leap over.

Group Practices

Small ball with a partner

Pupils can simply create a co-operative practice, throwing and catching in some way, or they can make a little, competitive 1 v 1 game which involves them deciding how to score and how to re-start after a score, e.g. one partner counts his or her throws and catches on the spot while the other partner races to touch a mark on the playground, ideally about a 15-metre run. When runner comes back, the counting partner stops counting and tells partner how many catches were made. Change duties and the new thrower and catcher try for a better score.

Skipping rope each

Free practice with a skipping rope lets pupils continue with the earlier practising, including trying skipping with the overhead pull, or activities with the rope on the ground.

Partners: one hoop and five beanbags

Partners 'take turns' at throwing five beanbags to try to land them in the hoop, which is 2 or 3 metres away. The secret of good aiming is to use a long, straight arm action to throw high enough to let the beanbag 'see' the hoop.

Lesson Plan 8 • 30 minutes
April

Emphasis on: *(a) the athletic activities of running, jumping and throwing; (b) increasing body control and self-confidence; (c) enjoying experimenting with a variety of implements.*

Warm-up and Footwork Practices
5 minutes

1   Can you do a big high jump over a line and show me which is your jumping-off foot?

2   You don't need to run fast to jump high. Show me a nice, springy push and let your front knee reach up high.

3   Four lines relay. Partners stand side by side anywhere inside the lines of the teaching area. On signal, 'A' races to touch the outside four lines (two ends and two sides) of the teaching space, and back to touch partner 'B' who repeats the run.

Skills Practices: with beanbags
10 minutes

Individual practices

1   Walk, finding good spaces, throwing up low to about chest height; medium to about head height; and higher to just above the head.

2   Walk, balancing the beanbag on the back of your outstretched hand. Throw it up gently to catch it with the front of your hand. Can you do this balance–throw–catch using both left and right hands?

3   All on one side line. Throw underarm to make your beanbag go as near to the opposite side line as possible. Run after it. Take it on to the opposite line and repeat back to starting line. Use a long swing forwards, back, forwards and throw each time.

Partner practices

1   Stand very close to your partner, about a metre apart. Throw the beanbag to each other a few times. Now move back one step and throw again, about 2 metres apart, a few times. Have one more move back to about 3 metres and throw and catch carefully again.

2   Partners stand on opposite side lines. Using an underarm action, can you throw the beanbag to land in front of your partner on his or her side line? This long aim and throw is helped by a long swing forwards, back and forwards with a straight arm.

Group Practices
15 minutes

Free practice with choice of ropes, hoops, balls or quoits

Can you show me your favourite activities with one piece of equipment? Practise continuously by yourself to improve.

Partners with one beanbag at a rope or line 'net'

How long a rally can you and your partner make before dropping the beanbag? Throw with one hand to partner's two outstretched hands.

Partners with medium or large ball

Try to keep moving as you show me ways to travel with, send and receive your ball. Hands and feet are both important.

Games

Teaching notes and NC guidance
Development over 4 lessons

Games | Year R | Lesson 8

Warm-up and Footwork Practices

1   Encourage a springy upwards movement in high jumping with the feeling of lifting arms, head and leading knee straight up.

2   The feeling is of rocking up into the jump from a heel–ball–toes action in the take-off foot.

3   In four lines sprint relay race, partners both start and finish at the same place. Each of four surrounding lines of the playground 'classroom' must be touched with a shoe, before racing back to touch partner. To help teacher identify winning couples, children are asked to finish 'Standing side by side, still.'

Skills Practices: with beanbags

Individual practices

1   Throw up with one hand and catch with two, ideally at about mid-chest height where beanbag can be well watched. The three different heights give practice in judging the effort needed to achieve these different heights.

2   Walking, balancing, throwing and catching is an enjoyable example of 'joining skills together with increasing control.'

3   The swing 'forwards, back and forwards' of the throwing arm is important to achieve a controlled and repeating throw and aim at a target line. Sufficient height is needed to 'let the beanbag see the line' and carry it to the target.

Partner practices

1   Repeat the practising at one width several times so that your body can 'remember' how to do it at that distance. Move a little further apart and repeat, discovering how much more effort and height are needed this time. One more move back and a final practice, aiming, catching and looking very carefully.

2   The cross-court aiming at your partner's line develops accuracy through straighter throwing, and judgements of force and height needed to cover a set distance. Repeated practice aims to develop skill and 'muscle memory'.

Group Practices

Free practice with choice of ropes, hoops, balls or quoits

Free practice with a choice of implements is provided to enable more practice of skills that are enjoyed and can be practised almost non-stop to become even more skilful and satisfying. Teacher challenges can lead to greater quality and variety. 'Can you spin the hoop on parts of your body or on the ground?'

Partners with one beanbag at a rope line or 'net'

Co-operative throwing and catching of a beanbag over a 'net' is practised at about 2 metres apart only. Beanbag is carefully swung forwards, back and forwards each time, aiming at partner's hands, outstretched as a target.

Partners with medium or large ball

In sending a big ball to a partner, emphasise sending it a short distance, keeping in the allocated area always, not disturbing other groups. Neat, well-controlled, repeatable practising is looked for, with the ball seldom wandering out of control.

Lesson Plan 9 • 30 minutes
May

Emphasis on: *(a) working carefully and thoughtfully, almost without stopping, to practise to improve; (b) learning to judge force and height when batting a small ball by oneself and with a partner; (c) planning to link simple actions together.*

Warm-up and Footwork Practices
5 minutes

1   Run and jump over the lines without touching them. I would like to see long and high jumps, pretending each line is a low wall which you have to clear.

2   When I call 'Stop!' show me how quickly you can stand, balanced on tiptoes, on the nearest line. Stop! (Repeat.)

Skills Practices: with small bats and balls
10 minutes

Individual practices

1   Can you walk, balancing the ball on the flat bat?

2   Stand, hit the ball straight up a little way, let it bounce, then hit it up again.

3   Try to walk, using the bat like a big hand, striking the ball down just in front of you. Use your wrist only.

Partner practices

1   Can you try, both with a bat, or one with a bat and one using a hand, to strike the ball straight up between you, then let it bounce, then hit it up. Keep your best score of 'Strike it up, let it bounce.'

2   One with a bat and ball drops ball to let it bounce up and very gently bats it for partner to receive and hand back to batter. Have four or five hits each, very gently and slowly, 'feeling' how much power to give it.

Group Practices
15 minutes

Skipping rope each

Practise skipping, on-the-spot or on the move. If you are just learning, use a slow overhead pull to make the rope slide along the ground for you to step over. Use a very small turn of your wrists.

Bat and ball each

Can you plan to do something on the spot and something where you are moving? Be gentle with your hitting and use your wrists, not your elbows or shoulders. Watch the ball well, hitting it just in front of your eyes (illustrated).

Partners: hoop each

Can you show your partner some balancing, either walking on the hoop on the ground or in both hands? You can swing the hoop forwards and back, and from side to side.

Games

Teaching notes and NC guidance
Development over 4 lessons

Warm-up and Footwork Practices

1 To encourage flight, elevation and height, ask pupils to pretend that each line is a low wall to be cleared. This should encourage a good sprint into a long jump and a springy action into a high jump. Children can be asked to think about 'Which foot do you push off with in your high jumps and your long jumps?

2 A quick response to 'Stop!' is always a good exercise because it trains a quick response to a signal or instruction. With a good class there should be no more than a 2-second gap between 'Stop!' and all being stationary, balanced on tiptoes.

Skills Practices: with small bats and balls

Individual practices

1 Bat is held at mid-chest height, with a well bent arm for good vision and control.

2 Bouncing upwards to about head height is produced by a gentle wrist action. The elbow and the shoulder do not join in.

3 Little hands should hold the bat near to its face and the fingers can even spread over part of the back of the face to help the feeling that the bat is an extension of the hand. Ball is struck firmly enough to bounce it up to about waist level.

Partner practices

1 Partners stand within touching distance of each other, trying to make the ball bounce vertically between them up to about waist height. Bat, or hand, if preferred, strikes gently under the ball, 'feeling' how much force is necessary. One bounce between hits is the aim, but more than one bounce between is helpful.

2 This challenging practice for a Reception class needs to be at no more than 3 metres apart. Receiving partner needs to have both cupped hands reaching forwards, ready to catch, and to show partner where to aim.

Group Practices

Skipping rope each

Learner skippers can run around with rope in one hand and practise the turning action at one side, then move on to the long, slow overhead pull, with both hands, to make the longish rope land well ahead before sliding along the ground towards them to step over.

Bat and ball each

Bat and ball practice gives another opportunity to practise the skills which very young children find difficult. 'Feel' and hand–eye co-ordination are being developed. Success in making short rallies is a source of great satisfaction. 'I can do three! Come and see me!'

Partners: hoop each

As a balance to the individual and difficult rope and bat and ball practices, partner activities with a hoop allow pupils to co-operate, demonstrate and learn from each other. Balancing, bowling or skipping are big favourites.

Lesson Plan 10 • 30 minutes
June

Emphasis on: *(a) neat, controlled actions developed by listening well to class teaching; (b) practising in a well-planned way; (c) co-operating with a partner to develop good footwork and ball control skills.*

Warm-up and Footwork Practices
5 minutes

1   Follow your leader who will show you walking, running, jumping or other ways to travel. Watch the actions carefully and try to show me a little sequence of two or three joined together which you can repeat.

2   Now the other partner will lead. Keep together and listen for the number I call out (corresponding to one of the numbered areas of the playground). Let's see which couple is first, and last, to arrive in that numbered area. Number... two!

Skills Practices: with small balls
10 minutes

Individual practices

1   Throw up and catch with both hands well cupped, fingers pointing away from you. Can you catch the ball in front of your eyes and let your hands 'give' to stop the ball bouncing out?

2   Walk, batting the ball up a little way in front of you with one hand. Let it bounce up, then bat it again. Bat; let bounce; bat up.

3   Roll the ball forwards, run after it, crouch to pick it up with one hand. Turn and repeat back to starting place. This is called 'fielding' the ball.

Partner practices

1   Stand, facing your partner, about two big steps apart. Throw to your partner's cupped hands which should be reaching forwards as a target. Let your catching hands 'give' to stop the ball bouncing out again.

2   Can you and your partner stand close together and bat the ball straight up between you with gentle, careful strikes?   What is your best score?

3   Now roll the ball to your partner (4 metres apart) for him or her to bend down to field, pick up and then roll to you.

Group Practices
15 minutes

Partners: with quoits

Play one with one, throwing over a low rope 'net', or one against one, to try to make the quoit land on partner's side for a point. Throw with one hand, catch with two.

Partners: with small ball

Aim your ball to land between two marks, cones or beanbags, then bounce up for your partner to catch. Now try to roll it between the markers, for partner to field.

Partners: with bat and ball each

Can you balance your ball on your bat? Now hit it up two or three times, then catch it, still, on bat. Walk, batting ball down just in front of you.

Games

Teaching notes and NC guidance
Development over 4 lessons

Warm-up and Footwork Practices

1 Emphasise that the leader must give the couple good space to travel through, and try to visit all parts of the playground 'classroom'. Leader thinks ahead and should be able to say what two or three actions he or she plans to include.

2 A smooth linking of the actions is to be encouraged, particularly if there is an attractive variety, e.g. slow, straight leg running; lively, well bent knees, galloping; tiptoe walking.

Skills Practices: with small balls

Individual practices

1 Encourage class to look closely at the ball and be able to say something about it – its colour; texture; any markings, etc. – so that they are concentrating on it right into their hands.

2 Bat up, let bounce, bat up is done with a soft, gentle action in the wrist, 'feeling' how little force is needed to send the ball to the right height and distance ahead.

3 In fielding a rolling ball, we run to a position beside the ball, facing the direction the ball is travelling, with ball on good hand side. Crouch to pick it up. A common fault is to run sideways beside the ball to try to go past it.

Partner practices

1 Make sure partners stand very close together, almost close enough to touch outstretched, cupped hands. The 'giving' in the hands is easily practised at this close range, and can be the emphasis of the practice.

2 'Standing even closer, bat the ball vertically up between you with a soft, gentle wrist action. Aim to make the ball bounce up to about waist height of your partner for the next hit.'

3 'In fielding a ball rolling towards you, turn half to one side with one foot forwards, one back on throwing-hand side, and crouch down to pick it up.'

Group Practices

Partners: with quoits

Gently aim and throw over the low rope 'net', or paint line. Partner is only about 2 metres away with both hands reaching forwards to show thrower where to aim with one hand. The preparatory arm swing forwards, back, then forwards and throw, is important.

Partners: with small ball

Small ball partners practice is done at about 2 metres apart, to make the aiming and the catching more successful, more often. At this close distance the aiming will be an underarm action.

Partners: with bat and ball each

Three different bat and ball practices for variety. Balance ball on bat at chest height. Try gentle hits up a short distance and then try to catch the ball, balanced again. Walk, using bat like a big hand to hit ball down on to ground. In all striking, emphasise that the wrist is used to move the bat, not the elbow or shoulders, which produce excessively strong movements.

Lesson Plan 11 • 30 minutes
July

Emphasis on: *(a) demonstrating, as always, enthusiastic and vigorous participation; (b) demonstrating a positive attitude which implies 'These lessons are fun, interesting, exciting and good for us'; (c) displaying a pleasing end-of-year level of variety and quality.*

Warm-up and Footwork Practices
5 minutes

1   Show me good, quiet, straight-ahead running with body, legs, arms and shoulders all pointing straight ahead. (No side-to-side twisting action.)

2   Remember that good running is also quiet and you don't follow anyone. Run on straight lines, not curves.

3   Partners stand side by side down middle of court. On signal, one races to touch a side line, then races back to touch partner's hand as signal to race to touch other line. Repeat.

Skills Practices: with skipping ropes
10 minutes

Individual practices

1   On the spot, all turn the rope over your head with a long, slow arm action. The rope hits the ground well in front of you, slides towards you and you can step over it. All practise this way to learn skipping, and use only a small wrist action.

2   Those who are able to skip well can try travelling forwards with a running action to take you over your rope. Continue to make the rope land in front of you and slide towards you, slowly.

Partner practices

1   If you are both learning, try to stand side by side and do the slow, overhead pull together at the same speed.

2   If you are both good skippers, play follow the leader, keeping well apart and well away from all other skippers.

Group Practices
15 minutes

Free practice with a partner with choice of balls, hoops, quoits, ropes, bat and ball

Can you and your partner show me some neat, quiet actions with your choice of equipment? Do something simple that you can keep repeating.

Skipping rope each

Practise freely, on-the-spot or moving. Can you skip with a bounce, feet together and sometimes with a running action, one foot after the other?

One beanbag among three: 'Piggy in the middle'

Pairs throw the beanbag to each other, trying to keep it away from the opponent in the middle. Pairs must be no more than 2–3 metres apart to make good throws and easy catches.

Games

Teaching notes and NC guidance
Development over 4 lessons

Warm-up and Footwork Practices

1 The 'straight-ahead' style refers both to the look of the body and the pathways being followed, in good running. Emphasise here how the hands (and, therefore, the shoulders) reach forwards and back, straight. The class can practise running along some of the lines, with feet pointing along the line, and arms keeping parallel to the line.

2 The emphasis here is on the route followed. Always run in a straight-ahead fashion, with a direction change to a new straight line when you find yourself following another, or at a side line.

3 In side-line sprint relay, emphasise that pupils must touch on or over the line with a foot. Race can last for 'Four!' or 'Five!' or more side-line touches. At the end the teacher calls out the names of the winning couples.

Skills Practices: with skipping ropes

Individual practices

1 This slow-motion practice is with a rope that is quite long, coming up to chest height when you stand on it. Learn to do it on the spot, stepping over the rope slowly sliding along the ground towards you. Turning hands are at about shoulder height.

2 Progress to the same action 'on the move', still stepping over the longish rope sliding towards you along the ground.

Partner practices

1 Standing side by side, facing opposite directions, about 1 metre apart and keeping together in their 'Step over; step over; step over' is an enjoyable activity.

2 In follow-the-leader skipping, you must stay far enough behind the leader to avoid entangling him or her with your rope. Space between the pair and space for the pair are important.

Group Practices

Free practice with a partner with choice of balls, hoops, quoits, ropes, bat and ball

In free practice with a partner, the aim is for near continuous practice at something that needs two for its performance, co-operating or competing.

Skipping rope each

While it is free practice with a skipping rope each, the teacher will continually be praising good work, commenting on examples of variety, and challenging pupils to try something more adventurous, always in pursuit of a greater class repertoire.

One beanbag among three: 'Piggy in the middle'

The typical method of playing is to stand, far apart, and throw the beanbag over the head of the one in the middle. Try to keep the throwing pair only 2–3 metres apart, so that a good throw and catch are possible. The difficulty lies in encouraging the receiver to 'move sideways and forwards into a space' to receive the beanbag, unimpeded by the one in the middle. If necessary, ask the 'piggy' to be passive to help the throwers succeed.